W9-CYT-748

WordPerfect® 6
Quick Reference

Que Quick Reference Series

Margaret D. Hobbie
Bob Beck and
Gary Pickavet

WordPerfect 6 Quick Reference

Copyright © 1993 by Que® Corporation.

Library of Congress Catalog No.: 93-84127

ISBN: 1-56529-084-4

96   95   94   93   4   3   2   1

Interpretation of the printing code: the rightmost double-digit number is the year of the book's printing; the rightmost single-digit number, the number of the book's printing. For example, a printing code of 93-1 shows that the first printing of the book occurred in 1993.

Screen reproductions in this book were created with Collage Plus from Inner Media, Inc., Hollis, NH.

Publisher
David P. Ewing

Associate Publisher
Rick Ranucci

Operations Manager
Sheila Cunningham

Publishing Plan Manager
Thomas H. Bennett

Title Manager
Charles O. Stewart III

Product Director
Timothy S. Stanley

Acquisitions Editor
Thomas F. Godfrey III

Editors
William A. Barton
Don Eamon
Heather Northrup
Anne Owen
Joy M. Preacher
Colleen Totz

Technical Editor
Harriet Serenkin

Book Designer
Amy Peppler-Adams

Production Team
Heather Kaufman, Bob LaRoche, Joy Dean Lee, Jay
Lesandrini, Caroline Roop, Linda Seifert, Sandra Shay,
Michelle Worthington

Table of Contents

Introduction

WordPerfect 6 Quick Reference is a collection of the most essential commands and functions that are available in WordPerfect 6, assembled in a task-oriented quick-reference format. Use this book to learn specific procedures as you learn the program itself. Keep the book handy to refresh your memory on how to perform tasks you need to carry out only infrequently. Hints, reminders, cautions, and shortcuts are scattered throughout the book to keep you out of trouble or show you the easy way to perform many tasks.

This is the book to keep in your desk drawer for whenever you must perform a word processing task quickly. You can, for example, find in this *WordPerfect 6 Quick Reference* the last-minute help you need to enhance a report's appearance by dressing it up with graphics, tables, graphs, and fonts.

The *WordPerfect 6 Quick Reference* is not intended to replace comprehensive documentation. The book is more like an abridged dictionary of common procedures. Que's *Using WordPerfect 6*, Special Edition, and *WordPerfect 6 QuickStart* are good choices to add to your computer library for more detailed instructions.

Hints for Using This Book

WordPerfect 6 Quick Reference shows you how to perform necessary word processing tasks with step-by-step instructions for those procedures. To get the most out of this book, first take time to read the overview section and to familiarize yourself with the new version of the program. Then turn to the Task Reference section to learn a specific task. Tasks are alphabetically arranged for easy reference. Each topic contains a brief explanation of its purpose, followed by instructions. Alternative methods of performing tasks are provided if applicable.

Keep the following conventions in mind while using this book:

Underlined letters in menu commands and dialog box options, which represent keys you press to choose those items, appear in **boldface type**. Words or characters you type into a document or a dialog box also appear in bold.

On-screen information and messages appear in a `special typeface`.

If you see two keys separated by a plus sign—such as Shift+F1—press and hold the first key, press the second key, and then release both keys.

If you see two keys separated by a comma—such as F1, Enter—press and release the first key, and then press and release the second key.

A WordPerfect 6 Overview

WordPerfect 6 is a powerful word processing program that enables you not only to create documents, but also to format, lay out, and enhance those documents with graphics, graphs, fonts, tables, and columns. Many people use the program to desktop-publish newsletters and flyers.

WordPerfect 6 retains the excellent word processing features that WordPerfect users have enjoyed for years. The program also offers the following additional benefits:

- Enhances many features familiar to users of earlier versions of the DOS program.

- Adds features previously available only in WordPerfect for Windows.

- Adds features not previously available in any version of WordPerfect.

The following chart provides a brief summary of some of the new and enhanced features of WordPerfect 6.

New/Enhanced Feature	Summary
Auto Codes	If on, automatically places certain codes at the beginning of the page or paragraph.
Bar Codes	By default, automatically prints on envelopes or, in the case of windowed envelopes, on the letter itself.
Bookmark	Puts a place marker in your document so that you can go to another part of the document and then return to your previous position.
Button Bar	A menu bar of buttons containing commands and macros that offer a fast way to access features and perform editing tasks. You can customize the Button Bar for easy access to those commands and macros you use most often.

continues

New/Enhanced Feature	Summary
Coaches	Offers mini-tutorials to guide you through certain WordPerfect features as you create a document.
Document Display/Editing	Enables up to nine documents to be placed into separate editing windows, all of which can be displayed on-screen simultaneously.
Electronic Mail	Enables you to send electronic messages with attached files from within WordPerfect if running on a network under Shell 4.0.
Envelopes	Generates envelopes, complete with bar codes, at the end of a merged form letter file.
Fax	Sends a Fax file and cover letter directly to your printer or to your Fax modem for transmission.
File Manager	Takes care of necessary file maintenance, file Quick Lists, directory changes, and so on.
Fonts	Improved font handling enables you to use Adobe Type 1 fonts, AutoFont fonts, Bitstream Speedo fonts, CG Intellifont fonts, HP LaserJet bitmapped fonts, and TrueType fonts.
Grammar	Uses Grammatik to clean up grammar errors before you show your work to others.

New/Enhanced Feature	Summary
Graphics	Enables you to select, move, or resize graphics by using the mouse. Edits and prints with full WYSIWYG capabilities.
Graphics Printing	Improvements include higher resolution, watermarks, shading, fill styles, and support for color printers.
Help	Offers on-line, context-sensitive Help for any function, including an Index, a Glossary, a "How Do I?" feature, Coaches, and Search. The Tutorial and Workbook are located under Help for on-line lessons and practice.
Hypertext	Links text in a nonsequential manner to other sections of text in the document, to text in other documents, and to WordPerfect 6 macros.
Interface	Switches from Text Mode to Graphics Mode to Page Mode and contains such elements as pull-down menus, dialog boxes, scroll bars, Button Bars, the Outline Bar, and the Ribbon to speed up your work. Uses a mouse for increased productivity.
Keyboard Definitions	Offers many shortcut keys (function keys and keystroke combinations) for bypassing the pull-down menu system and includes options for WordPerfect 5.1 and CUA keyboard compatibility.

continues

New/Enhanced Feature	Summary
Macros	Features a new macro language and new play and record functions.
Outlines	Features collapsible outlines and an Outline Bar to enhance productivity.
Page Mode	Displays margins and substructures (such as page numbers, headers, footers, endnotes, and footnotes) with each page in a document editing window.
Print Preview	Provides a WYSIWYG (what you see is what you get) display of the document that is close to the actual printed page and can simultaneously display up to 32 pages on-screen for checking general formatting appearances.
Ribbon	Enables you to change such options as heading styles, columns, justification, fonts, point sizes, and tab settings from your document window without leaving the document.
Ruler	Provides a visual reminder of your tab settings and margins on-screen in your document window. You can choose to view or hide the ruler.
Save	Saves a document to disk without prompting the user to confirm the replacement of the existing version.

New/Enhanced Feature	Summary
Save As	Saves a file in another format or under a new name.
Scroll Bars	Enables vertical and horizontal movement of the document's image on-screen.
Sound Clips	Embeds a Sound Clip in your document to emphasize your point. Put one in your spreadsheet, and it reads back to you the numbers you record into it.
Subdivided Pages	Enables you to easily produce a booklet or trifold brochure.

Choosing WordPerfect Features

You can access all of WordPerfect's features by using the mouse and nearly all by using the keyboard. Using the mouse involves pointing to menu options and clicking. Using the keyboard involves the use of mnemonics (underlined letters) on the pull-down menus and in dialog boxes. The keyboard also uses *shortcut keys*—special key combinations that invoke program features or display dialog boxes without accessing the pull-down menus.

Using the Mouse

WordPerfect 6 offers total mouse support. If you do not yet have a mouse, consider investing in one; a mouse can speed up your work significantly. Without a mouse, you cannot use Button Bars or the Ribbon, two features new to WordPerfect 6.

The following terms apply to using a mouse in WordPerfect 6:

Term	Definition
Mouse	Any pointing device used to move the screen pointer across the screen.
Mouse Button	The pointing-device button under the user's index finger.
Click	Press and release the mouse button.
Double-Click	Press and release the mouse button twice in rapid succession.
Drag	Press and hold down the mouse button while moving the pointer across the screen.
Drop	Releasing the mouse button at the conclusion of a drag operation.
Point	Move the screen pointer to a specific menu or dialog box item or to a document location.

The mouse enables you to choose menu items easily by using either of the following techniques:

- Click the menu that contains the item you want to choose. Then click that item on the menu.

- Move the screen pointer to the menu that contains the item you want to choose. Press and hold down the mouse button as you drag the pointer down the menu to highlight the item you want. Then release the mouse button.

In Graphics Mode and Page Mode, the screen pointer appears as an arrow on-screen. In Text Mode, the screen pointer looks like a small rectangle.

Using Mnemonics

A *mnemonic* is an underlined letter (in Graphics and Page Modes) or a boldfaced letter (in Text Mode) in the name of a menu item or dialog box option. (Mnemonics may also appear as a number next to the item or option.) A mnemonic identifies the key to press to access a menu, a menu item, or a dialog box option. To use mnemonics to access the pull-down menu system and display the Ribbon, for example, follow these steps:

1 Choose the View menu by pressing Alt+V.

2 Choose Ribbon by pressing I. (Press Esc to close the menu without making a selection.)

Alternatively, press Alt+= to access the pull-down menu bar, and use the arrow keys to move the highlight bar through the menu system. Press Enter to choose an item.

> ### Tip
>
> Choose View, Screen Setup; or press Ctrl+F3, Shift+F1. Then choose Screen Options, Alt key. This configures WordPerfect so that you need press only the Alt key to access the pull-down menus.

Using Shortcut Keys

Touch/speed typists usually find shortcut keys the quickest and easiest way to use program functions. WordPerfect offers more than 60 key combinations that bypass the pull-down menus and directly access its features and dialog boxes. The shortcut keys that involve function keys are listed at the appropriate locations throughout this book. The following table, however, lists the shortcut keys that use the Ctrl key plus a character key.

Shortcut Key	Function
Ctrl+A	Display the Compose dialog box.
Ctrl+B	Toggle bold font attribute on/off.
Ctrl+C	Copy a block of text.
Ctrl+D	Dictate a Sound Clip into a document.
Ctrl+F	Find a Quickmark.
Ctrl+I	Toggle italics font attribute on/off.
Ctrl+N	Discontinue all font attributes and revert to using normal font.
Ctrl+O	Toggle Outline edit and text.
Ctrl+P	Insert a page number (formatted).
Ctrl+Q	Set a Quickmark.
Ctrl+R	Access the Repeat dialog box.
Ctrl+S	Play a Sound Clip in a document.
Ctrl+T	Toggle Normal Text/Outline item.
Ctrl+U	Toggle underlining on/off.
Ctrl+V	Paste text from buffer into a document.
Ctrl+W	WP Characters.
Ctrl+X	Cut text from a document.
Ctrl+Y	Cycle through the active document windows.
Ctrl+Z	Undo the last action.

Document Windows

In WordPerfect 6, you can open a total of nine document editing windows, one on top of another or side by side, and then switch back and forth among these open documents. As with so many of its features, WordPerfect offers several ways to open a document window. The following two methods, however, are the most common:

- Choose File, New; or press Shift+F10.

- Choose Window, Switch To; or press F3. Choose the mnemonic number of the editing window you want opened.

Press Esc to cancel without making a selection.

Menu Bar

WordPerfect displays its *menu bar* at the top of the screen. This bar contains pull-down menus for accessing WordPerfect's features and functions. Choosing a menu option that ends with an ellipsis (. . .) displays a dialog box containing new options. Choosing a menu option that ends with a right-pointing triangle accesses another pull-down menu containing additional options.

Tip

You can shut off the display of Word-Perfect's pull-down menus to give you a larger editing screen. Choose View, Screen Setup; or press Ctrl+F3, Shift+F1. Then choose Screen Options, Pull-Down Menus to configure WordPerfect to hide the menu bar. (Choosing the Pull-Down Menus option again redisplays the menu bar.)

Title Bar

If WordPerfect displays a document in a framed editing window, the *title bar* at the top of the window lists the name of the document in which you are currently working.

┌─ **Shortcut** ─────────────────────────────┐

Choose **V**iew, Scree**n** Setup; or press
Ctrl+F3, Shift+F1. Then choose **W**indow
Options, **F**ramed Windows to configure
WordPerfect to display documents in
framed editing windows.

└──┘

Scroll Bars

If a document exceeds the boundaries of its editing
window, *scroll bars* enable you to move up and down
and side to side within the window to view all the
document's text. WordPerfect incorporates separate
screen-setup options for displaying the vertical and
horizontal scroll bars in Text and Graphics modes.

The vertical scroll bar appears at the right edge of the
screen and contains an up arrow at the top of the bar, a
down arrow at the bottom, and a sliding scroll box in
between. The horizontal scroll bar is identical in appearance to the vertical scroll bar except that the horizontal
scroll bar is displayed across the bottom edge of the
screen and has arrows at either end that point to the left
or right.

The scroll box changes size dynamically and acts as a
visual indicator of the amount of scrolling required to
reach each end of the scroll bar. Generally, the larger
the scroll box, the smaller the distance required to
scroll from one end of the document to the other.

To display the scroll bars temporarily

Choose **V**iew, **V**ertical Scroll Bar or **H**orizontal Scroll
Bar.

The **V**iew menu closes and the scroll bar you chose
appears in the editing window. You can remove the
scroll bar by accessing the **V**iew menu and choosing the
appropriate scroll bar again. If you open a new document, no scroll bars appear unless you choose them
from the **V**iew menu.

To display the scroll bars permanently

Choose View, Screen Setup; or press Ctrl+F3, Shift+F1. In the Setup dialog box, choose Window Options, and then choose Vert. Scroll Bar (Graphics), Vert. Scroll Bar (Text), Hor. Scroll Bar (Graphics), or Hor. Scroll Bar (Text). Finally, press Home, F7. This configures WordPerfect to display the vertical or horizontal scroll bars permanently in the different video modes. The next time you open a document, WordPerfect displays the scroll bar (or bars) in the video mode you chose.

To use the scroll bars

You can use any of the following methods to move up and down in a document by using the vertical scroll bar:

Click	To Move Document
The up or down arrow	One line closer to the top or bottom margin.
The left or right arrow	One character to the left or right, if cursor is not near the left or right margin. If cursor is at the left or right edge of the screen, approximately one-half inch left or right.
The scroll bar between a scroll arrow and the scroll box	One screen up, down, left, or right.
Any arrow and hold down the mouse button	Continuously up, down, left, or right until the cursor reaches the margin.
On the scroll box and drag	Up, down, left, or right until the cursor reaches the margin.

Status Line

The *status line* at the bottom of the screen displays information about the editing window. In all video modes, the right side of the status line lists information about the cursor's location in the active editing window and whether Caps Lock is active. In Text Mode only, the status line displays additional items of information, as described in the following table.

Item	Information Conveyed
Doc	Number of the active document editing window in which the cursor is located. *Value:* 1 through 9.
Pg	Number of the virtual page on which the cursor is located. *Value:* 1 through unlimited.
Ln	Vertical location of the cursor on the current page. *Value:* 0 to unlimited.
Pos	Horizontal location of the cursor on the current page. *Value:* 0 to unlimited. Pos changes to POS if the Caps Lock key is active. In Text Mode: • Pos blinks if NumLock is active until a key is pressed. • The Pos value appears in the font attribute colors for attributes active at the cursor's location.
Cell	Cell address if the cursor is located within a table. *Value:* A1 to BL32766.
Col	Column number if the cursor is located within a table. *Value:* 1 to 24.

The information displayed at the left side of the status line depends on its configuration setting. To display the options, choose **V**iew, Scree**n** Setup; or press Ctrl+F3, Shift+F1. Then choose **W**indow Options, **S**tatus Line to display a drop-down list of options for the left side of the status line.

Accepting the default **F**ilename option displays on the status line the name of the font active at the cursor's location until the document is saved as a file on disk. Choosing the F**o**nt option always displays the name of the font that is active at the cursor's location. Choosing the **N**one option displays no information on the status line at the left side.

Dialog Boxes

The primary function of a *dialog box* is to enable you to choose options that instruct WordPerfect how to use its features and options. A secondary function is to display information, messages, and warnings. Dialog boxes usually appear after you choose any pull-down menu item followed by an ellipsis (. . .) or press a shortcut-key combination.

To use the mouse to navigate through a dialog box

You can use the following mouse techniques within a dialog box:

- Choose options by moving the screen pointer to the option and clicking the mouse button.

- To enter text into text boxes, move the screen pointer to the text box, click the mouse button, and type the text.

- Click a menu or list name and hold down the mouse button. Move the screen pointer down the pull-down menu or pop-out list that appears, and high-light an option. Release the mouse button.

- Move the screen pointer to the check box of an option that you want to toggle on or off. Click the mouse button. An "X" in the box indicates that an option is on (or selected). To turn off (or deselect) a checked item, remove the X by clicking the check box again. More than one check box within an option group can contain an X at the same time.

- Click the option button next to an option you want to choose in a set of options. Option buttons are small circles that display a filled circle instead of an X if the option is active. Only one option in a group of option buttons can be active at a time. Choosing a new option button simultaneously deselects a previously chosen button.

- Click OK or Close (as appropriate) to close the dialog box and save and activate the options.

- Click Cancel to close the dialog box without making a selection or to abandon any changes made to options in the dialog box.

To use the keyboard to navigate through a dialog box

You can use the following keyboard techniques within a dialog box:

- As the dialog box opens, WordPerfect usually places the cursor on the first item in the box (sometimes called the *focus*). Press Tab to move the focus to a different option adjacent to or below the option containing the focus.

- Press Shift+Tab to move the focus back to a different option adjacent to or above the option containing the focus.

- Press an option's mnemonic letter or number to select or deselect a check box, choose an option button, or display another dialog box if the option is followed by an ellipsis (. . .). You also can press Tab to move the focus to the option and then press the spacebar or Enter to choose the option.

- Use the up-, down-, left-, or right-arrow keys to move the highlight bar in a list box or to move the focus around within a set of options in a list or in an area of the dialog box.

- Press Enter if the focus is on an OK or Close button (as appropriate) to close the dialog box and save and activate the options.

- Press Esc to close the dialog box without making a selection.

Keyboard Techniques

Although using a mouse is often the easiest way to move through WordPerfect, you also can navigate through your document by using the keyboard. Use the following keys to move around within the document:

Keystroke	Action
Home, ←	Cursor moves to beginning of the line.
Home, Home, ←	Cursor moves to beginning of the line, before any formatting codes.
End	Cursor moves to end of the line.
Home, →	Cursor moves to end of the line.
Home, Home, Home, ↑	Cursor moves to top line of the document, before any formatting codes.
Home, Home, ↑	Cursor moves to the top line of the document, after formatting codes, if any, but before the first character.
Home, Home, ↓	Cursor moves to end of the document.
↑	Cursor moves up one line.
↓	Cursor moves down one line.
←	Cursor moves left one character.

continues

Keystroke	Action
→	Cursor moves right one character.
Ctrl+←	Cursor moves left one word.
Ctrl+→	Cursor moves right one word.
Ctrl+↑	Cursor moves to the beginning of the paragraph in which the cursor is located. If the cursor is at the beginning of a paragraph, it moves to the beginning of the preceding paragraph.
Ctrl+↓	Cursor moves to the beginning of the paragraph following that in which the cursor is located.
PgUp	Cursor moves up one page.
PgDn	Cursor moves down one page.
+ (on numeric keypad)	Cursor moves down one screen.
– (on numeric keypad)	Cursor moves up one screen.

Task Reference

The following section is a task-oriented alphabetical collection of tasks and procedures in WordPerfect. Step-by-step instructions appear under the appropriate headings.

 Adding Text

Enables you to add text to a document that already contains text. Two modes are available for adding text: Insert and Typeover.

Insert Mode

Adds new text at the cursor's location. Existing text moves forward to make room for new text.

To add text in Insert mode

1 Move the cursor to the location in the document where you want to add text.

2 Type the new text. Existing text moves to the right and down.

Typeover Mode

Replaces existing text with new text that you type. Existing text does not move forward in this mode. If you type **too** but you mean to type **two**, for example, choose Typeover mode to replace the first *o* in *two* with a *w*.

To type over existing text in Typeover mode

1 Move the cursor to the location in the document where you want the new text to begin.

2 Press the Ins key to toggle from Insert mode to Typeover mode.

3 Type the new text over the old text.

4 Press Ins again to toggle back to Insert mode.

Advance

Moves text to a different position on the page. You can advance text up, down, left, or right.

Advance enables you to place text relative to the cursor's location or to the top and right edges of the page. This feature is particularly useful for placing graphics or text boxes on a page. You also can use the feature to fill in preprinted forms.

To advance text or graphics

1 Choose **Layout**; or press Shift+F8. Choose **O**ther, **A**dvance.

2 Use the mouse or keyboard to choose an option.

3 Type a measurement in the text box next to the option name.

4 Choose OK twice to return the program to the document's editing window.

Shortcut

Press Home, F7. This shortcut key combination closes a dialog box or menu and immediately returns to the document's editing window, even if are several levels deep into WordPerfect's dialog box or menu structures.

Auto Code Placement

Automatically places formatting codes at the beginning of a page or paragraph, depending on the codes selected.

To turn Auto Code Placement off and on

1 Choose File, Setup; or press Shift+F1.

2 Choose Environment, Auto Code Placement.

(The X in the check box next to Auto Code Placement indicates the option is active. Selecting the check box turns off the option. To toggle Auto Code Placement back on, select it again.)

3 Choose OK to close the dialog box and save the new configuration setting. (If you accessed Setup by using Shift+F1 in step 1, you also must choose Close. Alternatively, you can exit the Environment dialog box and return directly to the document by pressing Home, F7.)

On installation, WordPerfect defaults to Auto Code Placement activated. Codes that format pages automatically are placed at the top of the page, regardless of the cursor's location on the page; these codes format the page. Codes that control paragraph formatting automatically are placed at the beginning of the paragraph in which the cursor is located; these codes format the paragraph.

If Auto Code Placement is off, WordPerfect inserts a temporary hard return—[THRt]—at the cursor's location, followed by the formatting code. A page code controls the formatting of all pages after the current page. A paragraph code controls the formatting of all text that follows the code.

Backup

Regularly creates backup copies of the documents in each of WordPerfect's nine editing windows. By saving each document as a special file on disk, the Timed Backup feature protects your data from loss caused by program crashes and power failures. The program defaults to this feature being active and creates backup files every 10 minutes in the directory that contains the WordPerfect executable files—usually C:\WP60.

Original Document Backup offers protection from accidentally replacing a document you didn't mean to replace. The program defaults to leaving this feature inactive. Original Document Backup files are saved in the same directory as the original file, using the original file's primary name but with a **BK!** extension.

To configure Timed Backup

1 Choose File, Setup; or press Shift+F1.

2 Choose Environment, Backup Options.

3 From the Backup dialog box, choose Timed Document Backup.

4 Enter a numeric value in the text field beside Minutes Between Backups.

5 Choose OK twice to close the dialog box and save the new Backup setting. (If you accessed Setup by using Shift+F1 in step 1, you also must choose Close. Alternatively, exit the Backup dialog box by pressing Home, F7.)

To designate a directory for timed-backup files

1 Choose File, Setup; or press Shift+F1.

2 Choose Location of Files, Backup Files.

3 In the text field beside the backup option, enter the name of the subdirectory where you want the backup files created.

4 Choose OK to close the dialog box and save the new setting. (If you accessed Setup by using Shift+F1 in step 1, you also must choose Close. Alternatively, exit the Location of Files dialog box by pressing Home, F7.)

To turn on Original Document Backup

1 Choose File, Setup; or press Shift+F1.

2 Choose Environment, Backup Options.

3 From the Backup dialog box, choose Backup Original Document (.BK!) on Save or Exit.

4 Choose OK twice to close the Backup dialog box and save the new settings. (If you accessed the dialog box by using Shift+F1 in step 1, also choose Close. Alternatively, exit the dialog box by pressing Home, F7.)

Basic Formatting

Enables you to change the default format settings for tabs, margins, justification, and so on to create individual documents with a different appearance. Most of these settings are configured by using *initial codes* so that every document you open has the new defaults. You also can set them differently for just one document. Instructions given in the following sections change settings temporarily for the document you are currently writing.

Document Margins

Determines the boundaries for placing text on the page. You can set the top, bottom, left, and right margins. The default margins are one inch around the entire page.

To change document margins

1 Choose **L**ayout; or press Shift+F8. Choose **M**argins. WordPerfect displays the Margins Format dialog box, which includes the following options for setting the document margins: **L**eft Margin, **R**ight Margin, **T**op Margin, and **B**ottom Margin.

2 Choose the setting you want to change, and type a new measurement value in the text box adjacent to it.

3 Make any other changes to the other document margins by repeating steps 1 and 2.

4 Choose OK twice to close the Margin Format dialog box and save the new settings. (If you accessed the Margins feature by using Shift+F8 in step 1, you also must choose Close. Alternatively, exit the dialog box by pressing Home, F7.)

Paragraph Margins

Enables you to designate the left and right boundaries for paragraphs as separate values relative to the left and right page margins. You also can set a default value for indenting the first line of each paragraph and the amount of spacing that WordPerfect automatically inserts between paragraphs after you press Enter. The default values for the paragraph options are as follows:

• Margin adjustments are 0 (paragraphs use the left and right margins defined for the page).

- First-line indent is 0 (first line uses the left margin defined for the page).

- Paragraph spacing is 1.0 (pressing Enter moves the cursor down one line).

To change first-line indent or paragraph spacing

1 Choose **L**ayout; or press Shift+F8. Choose **M**argins. WordPerfect displays the Margins Format dialog box, which includes the options **F**irst Line Indent and **P**aragraph Spacing.

2 Choose the setting you want to change and type a new measurement value in the text box adjacent to it.

3 Make any other changes to other options in the dialog box by repeating steps 1 and 2.

4 Choose OK twice to close the dialog box and save the new settings. (If you accessed the Margin feature by using Shift+F8 in step 1, also choose Close. Alternatively, exit the dialog box by pressing Home, F7.)

Tab Set

Sets left tabs, right tabs, center tabs, decimal tabs, and dot leader tabs, starting where you want the tabs in the document and spacing them as you specify. The default is Relative **L**eft tabs starting at the left edge of the page and repeating every half-inch.

Absolute tabs are measured from the left edge of the page and stay where you put them on the page, even when the margins change. *Relative tabs* are measured in relation to the left margin and remain a constant distance from it even if the left margin's location changes in the document.

Left tabs, the most common, indent to the tab stop, and text flows to the right. *Right tabs* cause text to flow left from the tab stop. *Decimal tabs* cause text to flow to the left until the decimal alignment character is typed; then text flows to the right. The default decimal-alignment character for the U.S. version of WordPerfect is a period (.). Use decimal tabs to line up columns of numbers.

Dot leaders work with left, right, and decimal tabs to create a row of characters leading to the first character or number typed at the tab stop. The program defaults to creating dot leaders that are periods separated by a space. This option is useful for creating phone lists and other long lists that require scanning from left to right.

To remove one or more tab settings

1 Choose **L**ayout; or press Shift+F8. Choose Line, Tab Set.

2 Click the ruler at the place where you want to clear a tab, or use the arrow keys to move the cursor to the setting's location.

3 Choose Clear **O**ne, or press Del, to remove the tab setting at the cursor's location.

Shortcut

Choose Clear **A**ll to clear all tabs and start over.

---

4 Choose OK twice to close the dialog box and save the new settings. (If you accessed **L**ayout by using Shift+F8 in step 1, you also must choose Close. Alternatively, exit the dialog box by pressing Home, F7.)

To designate one or more tab settings

1 Choose **L**ayout; or press Shift+F8. Choose Line, Tab Set.

2 Choose **S**et Tab, and enter the location for the tab stop.

Shortcut

Move the screen pointer to the location for the tab stop, and click. Alternatively, use the arrow keys to move the cursor to the location for the tab stop, and press Enter.

---

3 Choose the tab category: **R**elative Tabs (the default) or **A**bsolute Tabs.

4 Choose a tab type: **L**eft, **R**ight, **C**enter, or **D**ecimal.

5 Choose **D**ot Leader, or press the period, to set WordPerfect to use a dot leader for this tab.

6 Repeat steps 2 through 5 to place other tabs.

> ### Shortcut
>
> Choose Re**p**eat Every and enter a value to create evenly spaced tabs settings beginning at the location designated in step 2.

7 Choose OK twice to close the dialog box and save the new settings. (If you accessed **L**ayout by using Shift+F8 in step 1, you also must choose Close. Alternatively, exit the dialog box by pressing Home, F7.)

To designate the decimal-align character

1 Choose **L**ayout; or press Shift+F8. Choose **C**haracter.

2 Choose **D**ecimal/Align Character, and type the character you want WordPerfect to use for the decimal character.

> ### Tip
>
> Press Ctrl+W to display the WordPerfect Characters dialog box, which you can use to designate any of its more than 1,700 characters as the decimal character.

3 Choose OK twice to close the dialog box and save the new settings. (If you accessed **L**ayout by using Shift+F8 in step 1, you also must choose Close. Alternatively, exit the dialog box by pressing Home, F7.)

To designate a character and spacing for dot leaders

1 Choose **L**ayout; or press Shift+F8. Choose **C**haracter.

2 Choose **D**ot Leader Character, and type the character you want WordPerfect to use for the decimal character.

> **Tip**
>
> Press Ctrl+W to display the WordPerfect
> Characters dialog box, which you can use to
> designate any of the more than 1,700 char-
> acters as the decimal character.

3 Press Tab and enter a value for the spacing between the dot-leader characters.

4 Choose OK twice to close the dialog box and save the new settings. (If you accessed Layout by using Shift+F8 in step 1, you also must choose Close. Alternatively, exit the dialog box by pressing Home, F7.)

Justification

Controls how text lines are arranged in relation to the left and right margins and the center of the page.

Left justification (the default) aligns text flush with the left margin. *Right justification* aligns text flush with the right margin. *Center justification* centers text evenly between the left and right margins. *Full justification* arranges text between the left and right margins by expanding or contracting the spaces between words. *Full, All Lines* arranges text evenly between the left and right margins even when the line ends with a hard formatting code such as [HPg], [HRt], [HRt-SCol], [HRt-SPg], [THPg], [THRt],[THRt-SCol], and [THRt-SPg].

To choose justification

1 Choose Layout, Justification. Alternatively, press Shift+F8 and choose Line, Justification.

2 Choose Left, Center, Right, Full, or Full, All Lines.

3 If you accessed the Layout feature by using Shift+F8 in step 1, choose OK and Close. (Alternatively, exit the dialog box by pressing Home, F7.)

Alignment

Controls the placement of text on individual or multiple document lines. Most alignment options can align individual lines, paragraphs, and text blocks.

To insert alignment options from a menu

1 Move the cursor to the location in the document where you want the alignment to begin.

2 Choose **L**ayout, **A**lignment.

3 From the pop-up menu, choose one of the following options: **I**ndent →, I**n**dent →←, **B**ack Tab ←, Hanging Indent, **C**enter, **F**lush Right, **D**ecimal Tab, or Hard **P**age.

To insert alignment options by using shortcut keys

1 Move the cursor to the location where you want the alignment to begin.

2 Press the shortcut key for an alignment option, as described in the following list.

Shortcut Key	Option	Description
F4	Indent →	Moves each line in a paragraph one tab stop to the right of the left margin.
Shift+F4	Indent →← (Double Indent)	Moves each paragraph line in one tab stop from the right and left margins.
Shift+Tab	Back Tab (Margin Release)	Moves the first line in a paragraph one tab stop to the left.

continues

Shortcut Key	Option	Description
F4, Shift+Tab	Hanging Indent	Moves the first line in a paragraph one tab stop to the left and each remaining line in the paragraph one tab stop to the right of the left margin.
Shift+F6	Center	Positions text an equal distance between the left and right margins, or centers text on a specific point.
Alt+F6	Flush Right	Positions text lines even with the document's right margins
Ctrl+F6	Decimal Tab	Aligns each line of text on the decimal-align character (the default character is a period).
Ctrl+Enter	Hard Page	Starts a new page at the cursor's position.

Line Spacing

Changes the amount of space between lines separated by a hard-line code.

To change line spacing

1 Move the cursor to the location in the document where you want WordPerfect to change line spacing.

2 Choose Layout; or press Shift+F8. Choose Line, Line Spacing.

3 Click the up increment arrow next to the Line Spacing text box to increase the spacing value between lines by increments of 0.1, or click the down increment arrow to decrease the spacing value by the same amount. Alternatively, type a value in the text box, and press Enter.

Shortcut

On keyboards equipped with a second set of arrow keys—called the *enhanced arrow keys*—located between the numeric keypad and the alphabet-character keys, press Alt+enhanced up arrow to increase the spacing value in increments of 0.1, or Alt+enhanced down arrow to decrease the spacing value by the same amount.

---

4 Choose OK twice to close the dialog box and save the new settings. (If you accessed Layout by using Shift+F8 in step 2, you also must choose Close. Alternatively, exit the Line Format dialog box by pressing Home, F7.)

Line Height

Controls the distance between the top of one line of text to the top of the next line of text. WordPerfect defaults to Auto adjustment, which automatically changes line height to accommodate font changes.

To change Auto Line Height to Fixed

1 Move the cursor to the location where you want WordPerfect to begin using the fixed line-height.

2 Choose Layout; or press Shift+F8. Choose Line, Line Height, Fixed. WordPerfect displays the line-height value active at the cursor's location.

3 Enter the value you want WordPerfect to use for the height of all lines that follow.

4 Choose OK to close the dialog box and save the new settings. (If you accessed Layout by using Shift+F8 in step 2, also choose Close. Alternatively, exit the dialog box by pressing Home, F7.)

Hyphenation

Inserts a hyphen to break words that extend over the right margin of the page. The remainder of the word wraps to the next line. The Hyphenation feature defaults to inactive.

To turn on Hyphenation

1 Choose File, Setup; or press Shift+F1. Choose Environment, Prompt for Hyphenation.

2 Choose a hyphenation option—Never, When Required (the default), or Always—from the pop-up list that appears.

3 Choose Beep Options, Beep on Hyphenation to have the program sound a tone if you need to make a decision about the hyphenation of a word.

4 Choose OK to close the dialog box and save the new settings. (If you accessed Setup by using Shift+F8 in step 1, you also must choose Close. Alternatively, exit the Environment dialog box by pressing Home, F7.)

5 Choose Layout; or press Shift+F8. Choose Line, Hyphenation.

6 Choose OK to close the dialog box and save the new settings. (If you accessed Layout by using Shift+F1 in step 1, you also must choose Close. Alternatively, exit the Line Format dialog box by pressing Home, F7.)

Hyphenation Zone

Controls whether the program tries to hyphenate a word or automatically wraps it to the next line without hyphenation.

The hyphenation zone defines an area on either side of the document's right margin. The default values are 10 percent of the line to the left of the right margin and 4 percent to its right. If the word at the end of a line begins or ends within the hyphenation zone, Word-Perfect automatically wraps it to the next line. If the word begins and ends outside the hyphenation zone, the program chooses it as a candidate for hyphenation. If you define a shorter hyphenation zone, the program chooses more words for hyphenation.

To set the hyphenation zone

1   Choose **L**ayout; or press Shift+F8. Choose **L**ine, Hyphenation **Z**one.

2   Enter new values in the text boxes adjacent to the Left and Right options.

3   Choose OK to close the dialog box and save the new settings. (If you accessed **L**ayout by using Shift+F8 in step 1, you also must choose Close. Alternatively, exit the Line Format dialog box by pressing Home, F7.)

Block

See *Select*.

Block Protect

See *Select*.

Bookmarks

Places a code with a unique name into the document at the cursor's location. The Bookmark feature can return the cursor to this location almost immediately at any time.

To place a bookmark

1 Move the cursor to the location in the document you want the bookmark placed.

2 Choose Edit, Bookmark; or press Shift+F12. WordPerfect displays the Bookmark dialog box.

3 Choose Create. WordPerfect displays the Create Bookmark dialog box and offers the 38 characters following the cursor as a default descriptive name.

4 Choose OK or press Enter to accept the default. Alternatively, enter a descriptive name—38 characters maximum including spaces.

Note

If you use the Block feature to highlight text before invoking the Bookmark feature, the program offers only the characters highlighted in the block as the default.

5 Choose OK, or press F7. The program returns to the editing window and inserts a [Bookmark:<*descriptive name*>] code. If you highlighted text by using the Block feature, the program inserts a revertible-code pair that appears as:

`[+Bookmark:<descriptive name>]<text>[-Bookmark:<descriptive name>]`

Finding and highlighting a bookmark automatically

1 Choose Edit, Bookmark; or press Shift+F12.

2 Highlight the name of the bookmark you want the program to locate.

3 Choose **F**ind. If the bookmark was created by using the Block feature and you want the text automatically blocked, choose Find and **B**lock.

The program moves the cursor to the left of the bookmark code. If you used the Find and **B**lock option, the program automatically blocks the text marked by the pair of revertible bookmark codes.

Editing a bookmark

1 Choose **E**dit, Boo**k**mark; or press Shift+F12.

2 Highlight the name of the bookmark you want to edit.

3 Choose an editing option: **D**elete, **R**ename, or **M**ove.

A *QuickMark* is a special type of bookmark discussed later in this book.

See also *QuickMarks*.

Button Bars

Offers a timesaving method of using the mouse to access and use WordPerfect features, functions, and options or to run macros.

WordPerfect features several Button Bars you can customize by adding or removing buttons. You also can create additional Button Bars. WordPerfect can be set to display automatically Button Bars in Text Mode, Graphics/Page Mode, or all video modes.

To display the default Button Bar

Choose **V**iew, **B**utton Bar. Repeat this toggling procedure to hide the Button Bar.

To create a new Button Bar

1 Choose **V**iew, Button Bar **S**etup, **S**elect. WordPerfect displays the Select Button Bar dialog box.

2 Select the name of an existing Button Bar to use as a pattern for the new button bar.

3 Choose **C**reate.

4 Enter a unique name for the new Button Bar.

5 Choose OK, or press Enter. The Edit Button Bar dialog box opens.

6 After adding or deleting buttons, choose OK twice or press Home, F7 to save the new Button Bar and return to the editing window.

To add a menu item as a button

1 If the Edit Button Bar dialog box is not open, choose View, Button Bar **S**etup, **E**dit.

2 From the Button Bar list box, select the name of the Button Bar to which you want to add a button.

3 Choose Add M**e**nu Item.

4 Using the mouse or keyboard, display any of the pull-down menus on the menu bar.

5 Click the menu item you want to add to the Button Bar. Alternatively, use the arrow keys to highlight the menu item, and press Enter. The program creates a button for the menu item.

6 Repeat steps 3 through 5 to continue adding menu items from the pull-down menus.

7 Choose OK twice or press F7 to return to the editing screen. WordPerfect saves the Button Bar with its new buttons. Alternatively, choose Cancel or press Esc twice to abandon all changes.

To add a feature to the Button Bar

1 If the Edit Button Bar dialog box is not open, choose View, Button Bar **S**etup, **E**dit.

2 From the Button Bar list box, choose the name of the button bar to which you want to add a button.

3 Choose Add **F**eature. WordPerfect displays the Feature Button List dialog box, containing a scroll list of program features.

4 Using the mouse or keyboard, highlight the name of a WordPerfect feature. Choose Select.

5 Repeat step 4 to continue adding program features.

6 Choose OK twice or press Home, F7 to return to the editing screen. WordPerfect saves the Button Bar with its new buttons. Alternatively, choose Cancel or press Esc twice to abandon all changes.

To add a macro as a button

1 If the Edit Button Bar dialog box is not open, choose View, Button Bar Setup, Edit.

2 From the Button Bar list box, choose the name of the Button Bar to which you want to add a button.

3 Choose Add Macro. The Macro Button List dialog box appears and displays a scroll list of macros in the default macro directory.

4 Using the mouse or keyboard, highlight the name of a WordPerfect macro. Choose Select.

5 Choose OK twice or press Home, F7 to return to the editing screen. WordPerfect saves the Button Bar with its new buttons. Alternatively, choose Cancel or press Esc twice to abandon all changes.

To move a button

1 If the Edit Button Bar dialog box is not open, choose View, Button Bar Setup, Edit.

2 From the Button Bar list box, choose the name of the Button Bar from which you want to delete a button.

3 Using the mouse or keyboard, highlight the name of button to be moved.

4 Choose Move Button.

5 Using the mouse or keyboard, move the highlight bar to the location where you want the button to be moved.

6 Choose Paste Button to complete the move operation.

7 Choose OK twice or press Home, F7 to return to the editing screen. WordPerfect saves the Button Bar with the buttons in their new places. Alternatively, choose Cancel or press Esc twice to abandon all changes.

To delete a button

1 If the Edit Button Bar dialog box is not open, choose View, Button Bar Setup, Edit.

2 From the Button Bar list box, choose the name of the Button Bar from which you want to delete a button.

3 Using the mouse or keyboard, highlight the name of button to be deleted.

4 Choose Delete Button and Yes to confirm the deletion.

5 Choose OK twice or press Home, F7 to return to the editing screen. WordPerfect saves the Button Bar with the buttons deleted. Alternatively, choose Cancel or press Esc twice to abandon all changes.

To change the Button Bar's screen location

1 Choose View, Button Bar Setup, Options. The Button Bar Options dialog box appears.

2 Choose the screen location where you want the program to display Button Bars: Top, Bottom, Left Side, Right Side.

3 Choose OK or press Home, F7 to return to the editing screen, with the Button Bar in the new position. Alternatively, choose Cancel or press Esc to abandon the change.

To change how buttons appear

1 Choose View, Button Bar Setup, Options. The Button Bar Options dialog box appears.

2 Choose the style you want the program to use to display buttons: Picture and Text, Picture Only, Text Only.

3 Choose OK or press Home, F7 to return to the editing screen, with the Button Bar displayed with the
buttons' new appearance. Alternatively, choose
Cancel or press Esc to abandon the change.

To display Button Bars in different modes

1 Choose View, Screen Setup; or press Ctrl+F3,
Shift+F1. The Screen Setup dialog box appears.

2 Choose Screen Options.

3 To set the program to display a Button Bar in Graph-
ics and Page modes, choose Button Bar (Graphics).
To set the program to display a Button Bar in Text
Mode, choose Button Bar (Text).

4 Choose OK or press Home, F7 to return to the editing screen. WordPerfect saves the new configuration. Alternatively, choose Cancel or press Esc to
abandon the change.

To designate a default Button Bar

1 Choose View, Screen Setup; or press Ctrl+F3,
Shift+F1. The Screen Setup dialog box appears.

2 Choose Screen Options, Select Button Bar. The
Select Button Bar dialog box appears.

3 Using the mouse or keyboard, highlight the name of
the Button Bar to be used as the default.

4 Choose Select.

5 Choose OK or press Home, F7 to return to the editing screen. WordPerfect saves the new configuration. Alternatively, choose Cancel or press Esc to
abandon the change.

Cancel

Cancels out the latest action in your document. You can,
for example, use the feature to exit a dialog box without
making a selection.

To cancel the most recent action

Press Esc, or press both mouse buttons simultaneously.

Center Page

Positions a page's text an equal distance between the top and bottom margins.

1 If the Auto Code Placement feature is active, move the cursor to any location in the page with the text you want centered. If the feature is inactive, move the cursor to the top of the page.

2 Choose **L**ayout; or press Shift+F8. Choose **P**age and then choose either the **C**enter Current Page or Center **P**ages check box.

3 Choose OK twice to close the dialog box and save the new settings. (If you accessed **L**ayout by using Shift+F8 in step 2, you also must choose Close. Alternatively, exit the Line Format dialog box by pressing Home, F7.)

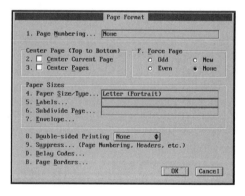

Clipboard

Acts as a temporary holding area in which you can store data you want to pass from document to document or

from application to application. (You must run
WordPerfect 6 under the WordPerfect Shell program to
use the Clipboard.)

The *Clipboard* is a memory buffer used for storing part
or all of a document. This feature can save you much
additional typing and formatting.

You can perform the following functions with the
Clipboard:

Save To

Stores part or all of a document in the Clipboard so that
the stored text is available for pasting into another part
of the document or to a different document in another
editing window.

To save text to the Clipboard

1 Using the keyboard or the mouse, highlight the text
   block you want copied to the Clipboard.

2 Choose File, **G**o to Shell; or press Ctrl+F1. The Shell
   dialog box appears.

3 Choose **S**ave To. The text block replaces the
   Clipboard's previous contents.

> ## Tip
>
> Use the Shell program's Screen Copy fea-
> ture, which has additional copy and retrieve
> options. Running WordPerfect under the
> Shell program also gives its File Manager
> feature additional copy and retrieve Clip-
> board options.

Append

Performs the same function as the Save To option
described in the preceding section except that the text
block is added to the Clipboard's contents.

To append text to the Clipboard

1 Using the keyboard or the mouse, highlight the text
   block you want copied to the Clipboard.

2 Choose File, **G**o to Shell; or press Ctrl+F1. The Shell dialog box appears.

3 Choose A**p**pend. The text block is added to the end of the Clipboard's end of contents.

Retrieve

Inserts data from the Clipboard into your document at the cursor's location.

To paste the Clipboard's contents into a document

1 Move the cursor to the document location where you want to add the Clipboard's contents.

2 Choose File, **G**o to Shell; or press Ctrl+F1. The Shell dialog box appears.

3 Choose **R**etrieve. The program inserts the Clipboard's contents into the document.

Close

Shuts documents, dialog boxes, and windows. If a document is in an editing window, this command closes the document and clears the screen.

To close a document

You can close a document by using any of the following methods:

- Click the Close button on the Button Bar.

- Choose File, E**x**it; or press F7. Choose **N**o or **Y**es, **N**o.

- Choose File, **C**lose, **N**o or **Y**es.

To close dialog boxes

How you close a dialog box depends on its button options, but most have a Close button you can use to exit the box. You also can use the following methods to close dialog boxes:

- Press Home, F7 to save changes and immediately return to the document's editing window.

- If a dialog box contains a Save, Save As, or OK button, choose one of these buttons to save any changes made in the dialog box and to close the box. If the dialog box does not close after you choose one of those buttons, and the box has a Close button, choose Close.

- If a dialog box does not contain a Save, Save As, or OK button, choose the Close button to save changes made in the dialog box.

- If the dialog box has an Insert button, use it to place into the document at the cursor's location any codes, styles, or other items specified in the dialog box. This button also closes the dialog box.

- To disregard changes you made to the dialog box and exit the box, choose the Cancel button or press Esc.

To close a window

Choose File; or press Alt+F7. Then choose Close.

Coaches

Coaches are an automatic Help system you can use with WordPerfect 6. Using dialog boxes and messages, a Coach instructs you through the steps required to perform a task, such as setting and finding bookmarks or enhancing text. A Coach provides helpful information for a task and even performs some of the steps of a task for you if you want.

Choosing Coaches

You can start Coaches from the Help menu or from any of the Help dialog boxes.

To start Coaches from the Help menu

Choose Help, and then choose Coaches. The Coaches dialog box appears.

To start Coaches from a Help dialog box

Choose the Coaches button from the Help dialog box. The Coaches dialog box appears.

Using a Coach

You can choose among several default Coaches that come with WordPerfect 6. WordPerfect Corporation offers additional Coaches to add to your copy of WordPerfect 6.

To select a Coach

1 Open the Coaches dialog box.

2 Select a Coach from the list of Coaches; for example, choose Bookmarks.

3 Choose the Select button.

The coach activates and displays instructions on-screen to perform the task you selected. Follow the on-screen instructions to perform the task. Watch for additional messages, especially if you are using the mouse.

Columns

Enables you to create columns quickly and easily.

To set up columns

1 Move the cursor to the document location where the columns need to begin. Alternatively, block the text to be placed in columns.

> **Shortcut**
>
> If you need to create newspaper columns quickly, use the mouse to access the Ribbon's Columns option

2 Choose Layout; or press Alt+F7. Choose Columns. The Text Columns dialog box appears.

3 Choose Column **T**ype, and designate an option: **N**ewspaper (the default), Balance **N**ewspaper, **P**arallel, or Parallel with **B**lock Protect.

4 Choose **N**umber of Columns, and enter a numeric value in its text box (the default is 2).

5 Choose **D**istance Between Columns, and enter a numeric value in its text box (the default is 0.5).

6 Choose Line **S**pacing Between Rows, and enter a numeric value in its text box (the default is 1.0).

> ### Tip
> Choose Custom **W**idths to display a dialog box that enables you to designate individual widths and spacing for each column.

7 Choose Column **B**orders to display the Create Column Borders dialog box.

8 Choose **B**order Style to display the Border Styles dialog box with a scroll list of styles.

9 Using the mouse or keyboard, highlight a border style from the list. If the style you want is not on the list, choose a different style library if any is listed as available at the top of the screen.

10 Choose **S**elect or Close to use the highlighted style.

11 Choose **S**elect to apply the style to the document.

To use columns

1 Move the cursor to the first column, and type the text for that column.

2 Press Ctrl+Enter to move to the next column.

3 After entering all text, place the cursor where you want the columns to end.

4 Choose **L**ayout; or press Alt+F7. Then choose **C**olumns.

5 Choose **O**ff.

6 Choose OK, or press Home, F7.

The following table describes how to move around in columns by using the keyboard.

Keystroke	Action
Ctrl+Home, →; or Alt+→	Move one column to the right.
Ctrl+Home, ←; or Alt+←	Move one column to the left.
Ctrl+Home, ↑	Move to top of current column.
Ctrl+Home, ↓	Move to bottom of current column.
Ctrl+Home, End; or Ctrl+Home, Home →	Move to last column.
Ctrl+Home, Home ←	Move to first column.
Ctrl+Enter	Inserts a column break.
Ctrl+A, Ctrl+Enter	Inserts a hard page break.

Column types

Newspaper columns read from top to bottom; text flows from the bottom of one column to the top of the next.

Balanced newspaper columns are newspaper columns in which the text is adjusted so that the columns are of equal length.

Parallel columns place text side by side, grouped across the page in rows.

Parallel columns with block-protect are similar to regular parallel columns, except that each row of block-protected columns stays together on the page. If one column in a row is long enough to move past a page break, the entire row of columns moves to a new page.

You can insert tables and graphics into text columns, and the text can be justified.

Tip

To edit heavily formatted columns, switch to Page Mode by choosing **V**iew, **P**age Mode; or press Ctrl+F3 and choose **P**age Mode. Choose **V**iew, Reveal **C**odes; or press Alt+F11 or Alt+F3.

See also *Ribbon* (for the easiest way to create Newspaper columns).

See also *Tables* and *Graphics*.

Comments

Inserts nonprinting comments into a document. The comments can be hidden or displayed and converted into printable text.

To insert comments

1 Move the cursor to the document location where you want the comment placed.

2 Choose **L**ayout, Comme**n**t; or press Ctrl+F7 and choose **C**omment. Then choose **C**reate. The program displays the Create Comment editing window.

3 As you type or edit the comment, you can enhance its text by using all the font choices, sizes, and attributes available on the pull-down menus and shortcut keys.

4 To save the comment and return to the document, click the `Comment: Press F7 when done` message or press F7.

5 The program displays the comment in a text box.

To edit a comment

1 Position the cursor below the comment.

2 Choose **L**ayout, Comm**e**nt; or press Ctrl+F7 and choose **C**omment. Then choose **E**dit.

3 Using any of WordPerfect's editing or formatting features, edit the comment.

4 To save the edited comment and return to the document, click the `Comment: Press F7 when done` message or press F7.

To turn a comment into text

1 Position the cursor below the comment.

2 Choose **L**ayout, Comm**e**nt; or press Ctrl+F7 and choose **C**omment. Then choose Convert to **T**ext. The comment's contents are added to the document as normal text.

To convert text to a comment

1 Using the mouse or keyboard, highlight the text block to be changed to a comment.

2 Choose **L**ayout, Comm**e**nt; or press Ctrl+F7 and choose **C**omment. Then choose **E**dit.

3 If necessary, use any of WordPerfect's editing or formatting features to edit the comment.

4 To save the edited comment and return to the document, click the `Comment: Press F7 when done` message or press F7.

To keep comments from displaying on-screen

1 Choose **V**iew, **S**creen Setup; or press Ctrl+F3 and Shift+F1. The Screen Setup dialog box appears.

2 Choose **W**indow Options, **D**isplay Comments.

3 Choose OK; or press Enter or F7.

To view hidden comments, repeat the steps for hiding a comment.

Compare

Enables you to compare two versions of the same document.

> **Caution!**
>
> Save a backup copy of the current document under a distinctive file name before using the Compare feature. You then have the original file in case you decide against keeping your editing changes.

To compare two documents

1 Open or retrieve the most recent copy of the file you want to compare.

2 Choose File, Compare Documents, Add Markings; or press Alt+F5 and choose Add Markings. The Compare Documents dialog box appears.

3 Type the path and file name of the file you want to compare with the document in the editing window. You also can use the QuickList or the File List to select a file path and name.

4 Choose Compare By and designate a comparison option: Word, Phrase, Sentence, or Paragraph.

5 Choose OK or press Enter to begin the comparison.

To remove markings

1 Choose File, Compare Documents; or press Alt+F5. Choose Remove Markings. The Remove Markings dialog box appears.

2 Choose Remove Redline Markings and Strikeout Text to remove all markings and return the document to its original condition.

Choose Remove Strikeout Text Only to keep the added (redlined) text in the document.

3 Choose OK or press Enter.

WordPerfect's Compare feature indicates deleted text by displaying it as strikeout text, which looks like text with a line drawn through it. Added text is indicated by redlined text. If text is moved, WordPerfect adds the message The following text was moved.

Changes found while comparing documents are marked in text, footnotes, endnotes, and tables, but not in graphics boxes, headers, and footers.

Immediately choosing **E**dit, **U**ndo or pressing Ctrl+Z removes any compared text and codes and restores the current document to its precomparison state.

Convert

Converts file formats to and from other programs so that you can exchange files with those programs.

To convert file formats

1 Choose **F**ile, **O**pen; or press Shift+F10. The Open Document dialog box appears.

2 Enter the name of the file you want to open; or use the File Manager (F5) or QuickList (F6) to locate and insert the file's name, and press Enter.

> ## Shortcut
>
> Click the down arrow or press ↓ to display a list of the four most recently opened or saved files. Double-click a file's name to open a file on this list; or use the keyboard to highlight a file name, and press Enter.

If the file is not formatted as a WordPerfect 5.x or 6.0 document, the program displays the File Format dialog box, which includes a scroll list of the more than 75 file formats recognized by WordPerfect 6.

3 Check the File Format text box to make sure that the file's format is listed. If it isn't, select the correct format from the scroll list.

4 Choose OK to start the conversion process.

> **Tip**
>
> The fastest way to scroll the list is to type
> the first letter of the file format you want.
> This moves the highlight bar to the first
> format that begins with that letter. Then use
> the up- or down-arrow keys to move to the
> exact format if it isn't the first one starting
> with that letter.

If the program does not have sufficient memory for
converting a large or complicated file from within
WordPerfect, it launches ConvertPerfect 2.0, the file
conversion utility that is one of the programs included
in the software package. After conversion is complete,
WordPerfect resumes operation.

> **Note**
>
> ConvertPerfect does not display a `Please`
> `Wait` message. Depending on the complexity
> of the document's formatting, conversion of
> graphics files or large files can take more
> than a half-hour—even on a fast system.

See also *Spreadsheet Importing*.

If a document has an existing name, using the Save As
feature instead of the Save feature enables you to save
the file in a different format.

See also *Save As*.

Copy

Inserts a duplicate of blocked text into a special memory buffer. The text remains available for pasting into
another location within the same document or a different document until replaced by the text from another

editing operation—copy, cut, or move—that uses the same buffer.

To copy a text block

1 Using the mouse or keyboard, highlight the text block to be copied.

2 Choose **E**dit, **C**opy; or press Ctrl+C.

┌─ **Shortcut** ─────────────────────────────┐

Press Ctrl+Ins for a copy operation that enables you to move the cursor and press Enter to insert the copy at another location within the document.

└──┘

To copy a block of text by using the mouse

1 Move the screen pointer to the first character or formatting code you want included in the block.

2 Drag the screen pointer to the last character or formatting code to be in the block.

3 Release the mouse button.

4 Move the screen pointer into the block and press the mouse button.

5 Drag the screen pointer to the location where you want the text copied. The screen pointer changes appearance to resemble a sheaf of papers.

6 Continue holding down the mouse button. Press and hold down the Ctrl key.

7 Release the mouse button and then the Ctrl key.

Counters

Controls how and when numbers appear in the document. This feature enables you to set values and insert codes. You can set this feature to automatically increment numbers so that each succeeding number is one larger than the previous number.

To create a Counter

1 Move the cursor to the location where you want the counter inserted.

2 Choose **L**ayout, Cha**r**acter; or press Shift+F8 and choose **C**haracter. The Create Character dialog box appears.

3 Choose **C**ounters. The Counters dialog box appears.

4 Choose **C**reate to open the Create Counter Definition dialog box.

5 In the **N**ame text box, enter a name for the Counter.

6 Choose **L**evels and enter a numeric value for the number of levels you want for multilevel Counters (the default is 1). Skip this step if you want only one level.

7 Choose Numbering **M**ethod and designate an option listed on the pop-up menu: **N**umbers (the default), Lower **L**etter, Upper **L**etter, Lower **R**oman, or Upper **R**oman.

8 Choose OK twice to close the dialog box and save the changed configuration setting; or exit the Environment dialog box by pressing Home, F7.

Cross-References

References a related topic in another part of a document.

The Cross-Reference feature inserts codes into the document to mark the reference and the target. The reference directs the reader's attention to another part of the document for information. The target is the location of the information to which the reader is directed. WordPerfect uses its Generate feature to keep track of all document references.

Tip

To help ensure accurate placement of codes, view the document by using the Reveal Codes feature—choose **V**iew, Reveal Codes; or press F11 or Alt+F3—while placing the cross-reference or target codes.

To mark both reference and target

1 Move the cursor to the document location where you want the program to insert the reference.

2 Type introductory text for the reference, such as **see page #**.

3 Press the space bar to add a space between the introductory text and the reference number.

4 Choose **T**ools, Cross-Re**f**erence, and the program displays a pop-up menu; or press Alt+F5 and the program displays the Mark dialog box.

5 From the pop-up menu, choose **B**oth; or in the dialog box, choose **M**ark Text, **B**oth Reference and Target. The Mark Cross-Reference and Target dialog box appears.

6 Choose Tie **R**eference To and designate the reference type you want inserted: **P**age Number (the default), **S**econdary Page, **C**hapter, **V**olume, Paragraph/**O**utline, **F**ootnote, **E**ndnote, **C**aption Number, or Counter.

7 Choose **T**arget Name and enter a distinctive name.

Tip

Choose Targets (F5) to display a list of target names currently being used in the document.

WordPerfect uses this name to tie the reference to the target when it generates cross-references.

8 Choose OK or press Enter. WordPerfect displays the document in the Mark Cross Reference and Target dialog box and prompts: `Position cursor and press Enter to insert target.`

> ### Tip
> Although there is nothing on-screen to indicate it, the program's Search (F2) and Backward Search (Shift+F2) features are available in the dialog box.

9 Move the cursor to the target's location and press Enter. The reference and target codes are inserted, and the page number or other reference type number appears at the original reference point.

10 Repeat steps 1 through 9 for every reference and target you need to mark.

After marking all targets and references, use the Generate feature to update the links between the cross-references and their targets.

To mark a reference only

1 Move the cursor to the document location where you want the program to insert the reference.

2 Type introductory text for the reference, such as **see page #**.

3 Press the space bar to add a space between the introductory text and the reference number.

4 Choose Tools, Cross-Reference, and the program displays a pop-up menu; or press Alt+F5, and the program displays the Mark dialog box.

5 From the pop-out menu, choose **R**eference; or in the dialog box, choose **M**ark Text, Cross-**R**eference. The Mark Cross-Reference and Target dialog box appears.

6 Choose Tie **R**eference To and designate the reference type you want inserted: **P**age Number (the
default), **S**econdary Page, **C**hapter, **V**olume, Para-
graph/**O**utline, **F**ootnote, **E**ndnote, C**a**ption Number,
or Coun**t**er.

7 Choose **T**arget Name and enter a distinctive name.

WordPerfect uses this name to tie the reference to
the target when it generates cross-references.

┌─ **Tip** ─────────────────────────────────┐

Choose Targets (F5) to display a list of
target names currently being used in the
document.

└──┘

8 Choose OK or press Enter. The program returns to
the editing window and inserts a ? at the cursor's
location.

9 Repeat steps 1 through 8 for every reference you
need to mark.

After marking all targets and references, use the Generate feature to update the links between the cross-
references and their targets.

To mark a target only

1 Move the cursor to the location where you want the
program to insert the target.

2 Type introductory text for the reference, such as
see page #.

3 Press the space bar to add a space between the
introductory text and the reference number.

4 Choose **T**ools, Cross-Re**f**erence, and the program
displays a pop-up menu; or press Alt+F5, and the
program displays the Mark dialog box.

5 From the pop-up menu, choose **T**arget; or in the
dialog box, choose **M**ark Text, Cross-Reference Target. The Mark Cross-Reference and Target dialog
box appears.

6 Choose Tie **R**eference To and designate the reference type you want inserted: **P**age Number (the
default), **S**econdary Page, **C**hapter, **V**olume, Para-
graph/**O**utline, **F**ootnote, **E**ndnote, **C**aption Number,
or Counter.

7 Choose **T**arget Name and enter a unique name.

WordPerfect uses this name to tie the reference to
the target when it generates cross-references.

> ### Tip
>
> Choose Targets (F5) to display a list of
> target names currently being used in the
> document.

8 Choose OK or press Enter. The target code is inserted at the cursor's location.

9 Repeat steps 1 through 8 for every target you need
to mark.

After marking all targets and references, use the Generate feature to update the links between the cross-
references and their targets.

To generate a cross-reference

1 Choose **T**ools; or press Alt+F5. Choose **G**enerate.
The program displays the Generate dialog box.

2 Choose OK, or press Enter.

Customizing WordPerfect 6

Sets up WordPerfect to suit your personal working style
and needs.

Installation

When first installing WordPerfect 6 on the system's hard
drive, you must answer some questions about how you
want the program installed.

Standard Install takes up about 16.5M on the hard disk but offers all the features contained in this sophisticated word processor. With this method, you can instruct WordPerfect to use Auto-Detect to determine the configuration of your system hardware.

Network Install enables you to install WordPerfect 6 on a network server with shared directories and then set up personal directories for each workstation.

Custom Install enables you to choose which programs to install and to specify the drive and directories on which they are installed.

Minimum Install takes up the least amount of hard disk space but leaves out some of the features. This installation is recommended only in situations in which disk space is very limited, such as on a laptop computer.

Update Install is for adding new printer drivers, installing a different printer, adding a new graphics card or sound board drivers, and so on.

Regardless of the installation option you choose, the fastest way to install WordPerfect is to copy all your disks to a temporary directory on your hard drive and then run Install from that directory.

To install from your hard drive

1 Create a temporary directory for installing WordPerfect by typing **md C:\temp** at the DOS prompt and pressing Enter.

2 Change to the temporary directory by typing **cd\ temp** at the DOS prompt and pressing Enter.

3 Put disk 1 of WordPerfect into drive A.

4 At the DOS prompt, type **copy a:*.***; press Enter.

5 After all files from disk 1 have been copied to your temporary directory, remove the disk from drive A, and replace it with disk 2; type **F3** and press Enter to copy all the files from disk 2 to your temporary directory.

6 Repeat step 5 to copy all the files from the remaining disks to your hard drive.

7 At the DOS prompt, type **install** and press Enter to proceed with the installation.

Starting WordPerfect 6 with Optional Switches

Starting WordPerfect 6 with various switches geared to your particular hardware and memory conditions enables the program to run more smoothly on your system.

To use a startup option, use the following syntax:

> WP *switch*

where *switch* is one or more of the startup switches shown in the following table.

Startup Switch	Description
/?	Displays startup options available with WordPerfect.
/bp=*buffer*	Creates a printer buffer in memory. *buffer* is a number from 0 to 63 specifying the amount of memory in Kilobytes (K) to use.
/cp=*codepage*	Specifies the code page to use with WordPerfect. *codepage* is one of the DOS codepage numbers.
/d-*path*	Specifies the directory path to store overflow files and temporary files. *path* must be an existing directory on your hard disk.
/dl	Disables the WordPerfect Launcher.

continues

Startup Switch	Description
/du	Prevents WordPerfect from using Upper Memory Blocks (UMBs).
/f2	Enables you to use extended text modes on your monitor.
/h	Same as /?.
/l=*langcode*	Specifies which text resource file (TRS) WordPerfect should use.
/ld-*path*	Specifies where the WP.FIL and TRS files are located. *path* must be an existing directory.
/ln	Enables you to change the license number.
/m=*macro*	Starts the specified macro when you start WordPerfect. *Macro* must be an existing macro.
/mono	Runs WordPerfect on a monochrome monitor.
/nb	If WordPerfect seems to be conflicting with TSR programs, use this switch to disable the WordPerfect Cursor Speed and Alt Key Activates Menus features.
/nd	Disables the "Shift-Key Sticking" fix.
/ne	Prevents WordPerfect from using Expanded memory.
/nx	Prevents WordPerfect from using Extended memory.
/nf	Use with windowing programs and if the screen goes blank.

Startup Switch	Description
/nh	Disables the initial Print to Hardware Port BIOS call.
/nk	Disables some incompatible Enhanced Keyboards.
/no	Disables the Keyboard Reset key (Ctrl+6).
/np	Disables the power down feature used with Laptop computers.
/nt=*netnum*	Tells WordPerfect which network operating system you are using.
/pf=*tempque*	Instructs WordPerfect to create temporary queue print files in the directory *tempque*.
/ps=*setup*	Specifies to WordPerfect the directory where the Setup file is located.
/r	Loads menus, error messages, and overlays into extended memory, if available; otherwise, loads into expanded memory.
/re	Loads menus, error messages, and overlays into expanded memory.
/rx	Loads menus, error messages, and overlays into extended memory.
/sa	Runs WordPerfect in stand-alone mode, even if you are connected to a network.
/sd=*prtfile*	Specifies the directory to create print files when running WordPerfect in stand-alone mode.

continues

Startup Switch	Description
/sp=*num*	Specifies WordPerfect to process print jobs for the length of time specified by *num*.
/ss=*r,c*	Specifies the size of your screen in *r* rows and *c* columns.
/tx	Displays WordPerfect in text mode.
/u=*uinit*	Specifies the initial for WordPerfect to use when creating temporary files. Specify this when running WordPerfect on a network.
/@u=*uid*	Changes the default network user identification to *uid*.
/w=*wrkspc*	Changes the workspace in RAM that WordPerfect uses. *wrkspc* is the number of K to use.
/wo=*wsovl*	Specifies the size of the WordPerfect workspace overlay. *wsovl* is the number of K to use.
/ws	Specifies the total amount of conventional and expanded memory available when starting WordPerfect.
/x	WordPerfect starts with the default setup values.
/32	Specifies that WordPerfect use the expanded memory specification version 3.2 only; not EMS version 4.0.

> **Tip**
>
> Create a DOS environment variable WP in your AUTOEXEC.BAT file to automatically use startup options from the preceding table. For example, to always load menus, error messages, and overlays into extended memory, or expanded memory if extended memory is not available, add the following command to your AUTOEXEC.BAT file:
>
> **SET wp=/r**

Setup

Choosing **F**ile, **S**etup (or pressing Shift+F1) enables you to customize various program elements such as **M**ouse, **D**isplay, **E**nvironment, **K**eyboard Layout, **L**ocation of Files, and **C**olor Printing Palette. You can run Setup from within WordPerfect any time you want to change one of these options. For more information on Setup, look up the particular item with which you want help. Keyboard Layout, for example, is discussed in the separate section with that name.

Use the *Mouse Setup* option to tell WordPerfect 6 about the driver for your mouse.

The *Display Setup* designates the Screen Type and Colors for all video modes—Text and Graphics/Page.

The *Environment Setup* enables you to set Backup Options, Beep Options, and Cursor Speed. By default, Allow Undo, Format Retrieved Documents for Default Printer, and Auto Code Placement are turned on. You also can choose when WordPerfect prompts for assistance in hyphenating a word (the default setting is never) and the Units of Measure the program uses (the default setting is inches).

You also can choose to have the program use the WordPerfect 5.1 keyboard—where F1 is the Cancel key and F3 is Help. You can even choose to have the program simulate WordPerfect 5.1 cursor movement.

You also can set up Delimited Text Options to configure
the program when you work with imported database
files.

To use WordPerfect's Writing Tools with documents
written in languages other than American English, you
need to install the WordPerfect Language Module for
that language. When these files are installed, use the
Environment option to designate the language.

See also *Backup, Auto Code Placement, Basic Formatting
(Hyphenation), Keyboard Layout.*

Use the *Keyboard Layout* option to select and create
keyboard definitions. WordPerfect 6 includes its Original
(WordPerfect 6) keyboard, an Equation keyboard (for
working with equations and the Equation Editor), a
Macros keyboard, and a WP52CUA keyboard (for those
accustomed to working in Windows). You can select a
predefined keyboard, edit it to suit your needs, and save
the customized keyboard under another name, leaving
the predefined keyboard intact. You can remap the
keyboard to assign function key commands and macros
to any key.

See also *Keyboard Layout.*

Location of Files must be set up and double-checked.
This is where WordPerfect looks to find its working
directories and programs. If WordPerfect can't find the
different locations containing soft fonts, for example, the
program's fonts features are of little use.

The *Color Printing Palette* enables you to choose from
several predefined color schemes, edit those color
schemes, and create custom color palettes.

The *Initial Codes* can be set to start every new document
with the margins, base font, justification, and paper size
you usually use. You access the initial-codes options by
choosing **L**ayout (or pressing Shift+F8) and then choosing **D**ocument.

See also *Basic Formatting (initial codes).*

Button Bars speed up your work by making frequently
accessed commands, features, and macros available

with one click of the mouse. WordPerfect ships with several predefined Button Bars, and you can set up and define other customized Button Bars for each phase of your work. You cannot use the Button Bar feature without a mouse. To access the Button Bar options, choose **V**iew, Scree**n** Setup; or press Ctrl+F3, Shift+F1.

See also *Button Bars*.

Screen Setup enables you to select various screen items as defaults so that they appear in your document window after you start up the program. These include horizontal and vertical scroll bars, the Ribbon and the Button Bar—with separate settings for Text Mode and Graphics/Page Modes. To access these options, choose **V**iew, Scree**n** Setup; or press Ctrl+F3, Shift+F1. To hide (or *deselect*) any of these items while working on a document, choose them from the **V**iew menu.

To select or set up a printer, choose **F**ile, **P**rint/Fax; or press Shift+F7. Choose the **S**elect and Setup (Shift+F1) options. Each choice displays dialog boxes that enable you to optimize how WordPerfect interacts with the printer.

See also *Printer Setup*.

Date Codes

Enables you to insert the date, the time, or both by using the computer's clock as document text or an automatically updated code.

Using Date and Time Codes saves much typing and editing. Suppose that you send out a form letter on several different days. Instead of reentering the date each day you send out the letter, you can use Date Codes to insert the current date automatically.

You can add a Date/Time code to a primary merge file. After you run the merge, the date automatically appears in the document.

The default date code appears as Month, Day, Year. If you prefer the date to appear in abbreviated form or as numbers separated by slashes (/), you must edit the codes in the Date Format dialog box.

To insert the date into a document

1 Move the cursor to the location in the document where you want the date inserted.

2 Choose Tools, **D**ate, Text; or press Shift+F5 and choose Insert Date Text.

┌─ **Reminder** ──────────────────────
│
│ For the Date feature to work correctly, the computer's internal clock must be set to the correct date and time.
│
└──────────────────────────────────

To insert date codes

1 Move the cursor to the location in the document where you want the date inserted.

2 Choose Tools, **D**ate, **C**ode; or press Shift+F5 and choose Insert Date **C**ode.

WordPerfect inserts a date code into the document. If you have set up time codes, these codes also appear in the document when you choose Tools, **D**ate, **C**ode.

To change the way the date appears

1 Choose Tools, **D**ate, Format; or press Shift+F5 and choose Date **F**ormat. The Date Format dialog box appears.

2 Choose the option button for one of the predefined date codes.

3 Choose OK or press Enter to accept the date code format. WordPerfect uses this format until you change it again.

To set up a time code

1 Choose Tools, **D**ate, **F**ormat; or press Shift+F5 and choose Date **F**ormat. The Date Format dialog box appears.

2 Choose an option button for one of the time format options.

3 Choose OK. The time codes selected remain in effect until you change the format in the Date Format dialog box.

To edit codes in the Date Format dialog box

1 Choose Tools, **D**ate, **F**ormat; or press Shift+F5 and choose Date **F**ormat. The Date Format dialog box appears.

2 Choose a code option and **E**dit. WordPerfect inserts the codes you choose into the Edit text box, from left to right.

3 Edit the codes to suit your needs.

4 Choose OK or press Enter to confirm the new format and return to the document.

Document Summary

Summarizes certain key information about the document.

WordPerfect 6 enables you to create a customized document summary with up to 54 information fields. The default *Document Summary* consists of a descriptive name and type, the author's name, the typist's name, creation and latest revision dates, subject, account, keywords to search for, and an abstract. The descriptive name in a document summary can be as long as 68 characters. If you use WordPerfect's File Manager, the

descriptive file names can appear in the QuickList.
Descriptive type enables you to sort your files by
categories.

If you need to create document summaries for most of
your documents, you must change your settings in the
Document Summary Preferences dialog box.

To define a custom Document Summary

1 Choose **L**ayout; or press Shift+F8. Choose **D**ocument, **S**ummary, Select Fields (F4). The Select
   Summary Fields dialog box opens.

2 Use the dialog box's options to create a customized
   summary form by adding or deleting information
   fields.

3 Choose Use as Default (F10).

To create a summary for a document

1 Choose **F**ile, **S**ummary; or press Shift+F8 and choose
   Document, **S**ummary. The Document Summary dialog box appears.

2 Choose Extract (Shift+F10), **Y**es. WordPerfect ob-
   tains the necessary information from the document
   and fills in some of the fields for you.

3 In the appropriate text boxes, type the information
   you want to appear in the document's summary.

4 Choose the appropriate buttons for what you want
   to do with the Document Summary—Extract, Save,
   Delete, or Print.

5 Choose OK to return to the document.

To create the Document Summary automatically

1 Choose **F**ile, **S**ummary; or press Shift+F8 and choose
   Document, **S**ummary. The Document Summary dialog box appears.

2 Choose Setup (Shift+F1). The Document Summary
   Setup dialog box appears.

3 Choose Create Summary on Exit/Save.

4 Choose OK or press Enter to return to the document.

Each time the program saves or exits a document, it displays the Document Summary dialog box.

To customize Document Summary information

1 Choose File Document Summary; or press Shift+F8 and choose Document, Summary. The Document Summary dialog box appears.

2 Choose Setup (Shift+F1) to display the Document Summary Setup dialog box.

3 Type new information in the Subject Search Text and Default Descriptive Type text boxes.

4 Choose OK or press Enter to return to the Document Summary dialog box.

5 Choose Select Fields (F4) to display the Select Summary Fields dialog box.

6 Choose the fields to be added from the Available Fields list box.

7 Choose OK to return to the Document Summary dialog box.

8 Choose OK to close the dialog box and return to the document.

To save the summary as a file

1 Choose, File, Summary; or press Shift+F8 and choose Document, Summary. The Document Summary dialog box appears.

2 Choose the Save (F10).

3 Type a file name in the Filename text box, including complete drive and path information if you are saving the summary to a different drive or directory.

4 Choose OK, and then choose Close.

Caution! ─────────────────────────────

Use a unique file name for the Document
Summary to avoid overwriting the file to
which it belongs.

To use Document Summary as an aid to searching for files

1 Choose File, Summary; or press Shift+F8 and choose
Document, Summary. The Document Summary
dialog box appears.

2 Choose Setup (Shift+F1) to display the Document
Summary Setup dialog box.

3 Type the Subject Search Text to use to search for
the subject. The default is RE:, but you can enter a
different keyword.

4 In the Default Descriptive Type text box, type a description that fits the type of files you most often
create.

5 Choose Create Summary on Save/Exit to instruct
WordPerfect to create a summary every time you
save a document.

6 Choose OK to save the changes, and then choose
Close.

If you use the File Manager, the descriptive file names
can appear in the QuickList.

If you entered text in Subject Search Text, WordPerfect
automatically extracts from the document that keyword,
as well as the words that immediately follow (up to 68
characters, including spaces).

To create document summaries for most documents,
you must change the setting in the Document Summary
Setup dialog box to Create Document Summary on Exit.

Enhancing Documents

Improves the appearance of a document, which can increase the reader's interest in what you have written. The following sections show you how to use these WordPerfect 6 features to enhance the appearance of your documents:

- borders (color spacing, shadows, and shape)

- fill styles

- bullets

- headers and footers

- watermarks

For information on other program features that you can use to enhance document appearance, see the sections on columns, fonts, graphic lines and images, line height, page margins, paragraph margins, spreadsheet importing, and tables.

Borders

Creates borders for paragraphs, tables, columns, graphics, and even pages. You can choose among predefined borders or create your own. WordPerfect automatically surrounds the paragraph containing the cursor—and all paragraphs that follow it—in one border defined by the border style you choose using the following steps.

To define a paragraph border

1 If the Auto Code Placement (ACP) feature is active, move the cursor to any location within the first paragraph that you want to be enclosed in a border. If the ACP feature is not active, move the cursor to the beginning of the first paragraph you want enclosed in a border.

Caution!

If the Auto Code Placement (ACP) feature is active, WordPerfect automatically places the paragraph border code at the beginning of the paragraph in which the cursor is located. If the ACP feature is not active and the cursor is not at the beginning of a paragraph, the program creates a temporary hard return code that splits the paragraph at the cursor's location and inserts the paragraph border code at the beginning of the next line.

2 Choose **G**raphics; or press Alt+F9. Choose **B**orders, **P**aragraph; or press Shift+F8 and choose **L**ine, Paragraph **B**orders. WordPerfect displays the Create Paragraph Border dialog box.

3 Choose **B**order Style. The program displays the Border Styles dialog box with the currently active border style marked by the highlight bar and an asterisk.

4 Using the keyboard or mouse, move the highlight bar to the border style you want to be the default for the paragraph border. Choose the new style by double-clicking its name, choosing **S**elect, or pressing Enter.

5 Choose OK to close the dialog box, activate the border style, and return to the document's editing window. (If you accessed this feature by using Shift+F8 in step 2, you also must choose Close. Alternatively, press Home, F7 to close the dialog box and return to the document.)

Tip

To return to the document's editing window *without* creating paragraph borders, close each dialog box by pressing Esc.

The program returns to the document's editing window and inserts a code that appears similar to this:

```
[Para Border:<style> Border;<style> Fill or [None]]
```

To discontinue paragraph borders

1 If the Auto Code Placement (ACP) feature is active, move the cursor to any location within the first paragraph that you do *not* want to be enclosed in a border. If the APC feature is not active, move the cursor to the beginning of the first paragraph you do not want enclosed in a border.

┌─ **Caution!** ──────────────────────────

If the Auto Code Placement (ACP) feature is active, WordPerfect automatically places the termination code at the beginning of the paragraph in which the cursor is located. If the ACP feature is not active and the cursor is not at the beginning of a paragraph, the program creates a temporary hard return code that splits the paragraph at the cursor's location and inserts the termination code at the beginning of the next line.

2 Choose **G**raphics; or press Alt+F9. Choose **B**orders, **P**aragraph; or press Shift+F8 and choose **L**ine, Para-graph **B**orders. The Create Paragraph Border dialog box appears.

3 Choose **B**order Style. The program displays the Border Styles dialog box with the currently active border style marked by the highlight bar and an asterisk.

4 Choose **O**ff. The program returns to the document's editing window and inserts this code:

```
[Para Border:[None];[None]]
```

> **Tip**
>
> To return to the document's editing window *without* discontinuing paragraph borders, close each dialog box by pressing Esc.

To define a border around specific paragraphs only

1 If the Auto Code Placement (ACP) feature is active, move the cursor to any location within the first paragraph that you do *not* want to be enclosed in a border. If the APC feature is not active, move the cursor to the beginning of the first paragraph you do not want enclosed in a border.

2 Using one of the methods described in the Block section (see *Select*), highlight a location in the last paragraph to be enclosed by the border.

3 Follow steps 2-5 in the instructions labeled *To define a paragraph border*, earlier in this section. At the conclusion of those steps, the program returns to the document's editing window.

WordPerfect inserts the code that tells it to begin the paragraph border at the beginning of the paragraph where the block began. This code contains a + that shows it is the beginning code of a revertible code pair. WordPerfect inserts the code that tells it to terminate the paragraph border at the beginning of the paragraph where the block ended. This code contains a – that shows it is the ending code in a revertible code pair.

To define a page border

1 Move the cursor to any location on the first page that you want the program to enclose in a border.

2 Choose **G**raphics; or press Alt+F9. Choose **B**orders, **P**age; or press Shift+F8 and choose **P**age, Page **B**orders. The Create Page Border dialog box appears.

3 Choose **B**order Style. The program displays the Border Styles dialog box with the currently active border style marked by the highlight bar and an asterisk.

4 Using the keyboard or mouse, move the highlight bar to the border style you want to be the default for the page border. Choose the new style by double-clicking its name, choosing **S**elect, or pressing Enter.

5 Choose OK to close the dialog box, activate the page border, and return the program to the document's editing window. (If you accessed this feature using Shift+F8 in step 2, also choose Close.) Alternatively, press Home, F7 to close the dialog box and return to the document.

┌─ **Tip** ─────────────────────────────────
│
│ To return to the document's editing window *without* creating a page border, close each dialog box by pressing Esc.
│
└──

The program returns to the document's editing window and inserts a code that appears similar to the following:

```
[Pg Border:<style> Border;<style> Fill or [None]]
```

┌─ **Caution!** ────────────────────────────
│
│ If the Auto Code Placement (ACP) feature is active, WordPerfect automatically places the page border code at the top of the page on which the cursor is located. If the ACP feature is not active, the program inserts the code at the cursor's location. Regardless of the code's location, WordPerfect begins creating page borders on the page containing the code.
│
└──

To change the corner style of page borders

1 Follow steps 1-3 in the section labeled *To define a page border* to open the Border Styles dialog box.

2 Choose **C**orners. The program displays the Border Corners dialog box.

┌─ **Note** ─────────────────────────────
│
│ The Corners feature is available only for
│ page borders.
│
└──

3 Choose a corner type: **S**quare or **R**ounded.

4 By default, the program uses 0.325" as the radius for the corners. This value produces a smooth round corner for most pages and usually does not need to be changed. If you want the program to use a different curve, choose the **C**orner Radius option and enter a numeric value in the option's text box.

5 Choose OK, Close, OK to close the dialog box, activate the page border corner style, and return to the document's editing window. Alternatively, press Home, F7 to close the dialog box and return to the document.

To discontinue page borders

1 If the Auto Code Placement (ACP) feature is active, move the cursor to the last page you want enclosed in a border. If the APC feature is not active, move the cursor to the first page you do *not* want enclosed in a border.

2 Choose **G**raphics; or press Alt+F9. Choose **B**orders, **P**aragraph; or press Shift+F8 and choose **P**age, Page **B**orders. The Create Page Border dialog box appears.

3 Choose **B**order Style. The program displays the Border Styles dialog box with the currently active border style marked by the highlight bar and an asterisk.

4 Choose **Off**. The program returns to the document's editing window and inserts the following code, which terminates the page border:

[Pg Border:[None];[None]]

Caution!

If the Auto Code Placement (ACP) feature is active, WordPerfect automatically places the page-border code at the top of the page on which the cursor is located. If the ACP feature is not active, the program inserts the code at the cursor's location. Regardless of the code's location on the page, WordPerfect terminates page borders on the page containing the code.

Tip

To return to the document's editing window *without* discontinuing page borders, close each dialog box by pressing Esc.

To define a border around specific pages only

1 Move the cursor to any location on the first page that you want enclosed in a border.

2 If the Auto Code Placement (ACP) feature is active, use one of the methods described in the Block section (see *Select*) to highlight a location in the last page to be enclosed by the border. If the APC feature is not active, use one of the methods described in the Block section to highlight the first page you do *not* want enclosed in a border.

3 Follow steps 2-5 in the instructions labeled *To define a page border*, earlier in this section. At the conclusion of those steps, the program returns to the document's editing window and inserts a code that contains a + to show that it is the beginning code of a revertible code pair. The code that terminates the page border contains a – to show that it is the ending code in a revertible code pair.

To add a column border

1 If the Auto Code Placement (ACP) feature is active, move the cursor to any location within any column that you want to be enclosed in a border. If the APC feature is not active, move the cursor to a location immediately to the right of the code that defines the beginning of the first column you want enclosed in a border.

Caution!

If the Auto Code Placement (ACP) feature is active, WordPerfect automatically places the column border code adjacent to the column definition code. If the ACP feature is not active and the cursor is not adjacent to the column definition code, the program creates a temporary hard column code at the cursor's location and adds the number of temporary hard column codes required to move the cursor to the beginning of the column at the left margin where it inserts the column border code.

2 Choose **G**raphics; or press Alt+F9. Choose B**o**rders, **C**olumns; or press Alt+F7 and choose **C**olumns, Column **B**orders. The Edit Column Border dialog box appears.

3 Choose **B**order Style. The program displays the Border Styles dialog box with the currently active border style marked by the highlight bar and an asterisk.

4 Using the keyboard or mouse, move the highlight bar to the border style you want to be the default for the current column and all that follow it. Choose the new style by double-clicking its name, choosing **S**elect, or pressing Enter.

5 Choose OK to close the dialog box and activate the column border. (If you accessed this feature by using Alt+F7 in step 2, you also must choose Close. Alternatively, press Home, F7 to close the dialog box and return to the document.)

Tip

To return to the document's editing window *without* creating a column border, close each dialog box by pressing Esc.

The program returns to the document's editing window and inserts a code similar to the following:

```
[Col Border:<style description>;<style> Fill or [None]]
```

To discontinue column borders

1 If the Auto Code Placement (ACP) feature is active, move the cursor to any location above or in the first column you do *not* want to have column borders. If the APC feature is not active, move the cursor immediately to the left of the code defining the first column you do *not* want to have column borders.

Caution!

Regardless of whether the Auto Code Placement feature is active, if you discontinue a column border definition with the cursor at any location other than inside of a column, WordPerfect inserts the code terminating column borders *and* a new column definition code at the cursor's location. If the ACP feature is inactive, you *must* place the cursor immediately to the left of a column-definition code.

---

2 Choose **G**raphics; or press Alt+F9. Choose **B**orders, **C**olumns; or press Alt+F7 and choose **C**olumns, Column **B**orders. The Edit Column Border dialog box appears.

3 Choose **B**order Style. The program displays the Border Styles dialog box with the currently active border style marked by the highlight bar and an asterisk.

4 Choose **O**ff. The program returns to the document's editing window and inserts this code:

```
[Col Border:[None];[None]]
```

Tip

To return to the document's editing window *without* discontinuing column borders, close each dialog box by pressing Esc.

To customize a paragraph, page, or column border

1 Move the cursor to a location inside of the text where you want to create the custom border.

2 Choose **G**raphics (or press Alt+F9), and then choose **B**orders. Then choose either **P**aragraph, P**a**ge, or **C**olumns. Alternatively, for paragraph borders, press Shift+F8 and choose **L**ine, Paragraph **B**orders; for page borders, press Shift+F8 and choose **P**age, Page **B**orders; for columns, press Alt+F7 and choose **C**olumns, Column **B**orders. The appropriate border dialog box appears.

3 Choose Customize. The appropriate Customize Border dialog box appears. If you choose columns, for example, the Customize Column Borders dialog box appears.

4 Choose **L**ines to display the Border Line Styles dialog box. Then choose Select **A**ll. The Line Styles dialog box appears.

5 Using the keyboard or mouse, move the highlight bar to the border style you want to be the default for the left, right, top, bottom, and separator border lines. Choose the new style by double-clicking its name, choosing **S**elect, or pressing Enter.

6 Choose Close twice to close the dialog boxes, save the new settings, and return to the document's editing window. (If you accessed the customize feature by using a function key combination in step 2, you also must choose OK. Alternatively, close all the dialog boxes by pressing Home, F7.)

To change the color of a border

1 Follow steps 1-3 in the section labeled *To customize a paragraph, page, or column border* to open a Customize Border dialog box.

2 Choose Color. The Border Line Color dialog box appears.

3 Select Choose One Color for All Lines. The program displays the Color Selection dialog box that includes the Palette Colors list box.

4 Using the keyboard or mouse, move the highlight bar to the color you want to be the default for the border lines.

5 If the program is in Graphics Mode or Page Mode and you want to change the color's hue, choose Shade (% of Color) and enter a numeric value from **0** to **100** in the text box. This option is not available when the program is operating in Text Mode.

Shortcut

The increment arrows—the up and down arrows to the right of the Shade option's text field—enable you to change the numeric value by using the mouse. Clicking the up arrow increases the value in the text box by 1 to a maximum value of 100. Clicking the down arrow decreases the value in the text box by 1 to a minimum of 0. Alternatively, on keyboards with a second set of arrow keys, called the enhanced arrow keys, located between the numeric keypad and the alphabet character keys, hold down the Alt key and the enhanced up arrow to increase the value in units of 1 percent, or press the Alt key and the enhanced down arrow to decrease the spacing value in units of 1 percent.

6 Double-click the text field or press Enter to display the results of the changed percentage in the color box below the **Sh**ade option.

7 Choose the new color by double-clicking its name in the list box. Alternatively, choose **S**elect or Close.

8 Choose OK, Close, and OK to return to the document's editing window. Alternatively, close all the dialog boxes by pressing Home, F7.

To adjust inside and outside border spacing

1 Follow steps 1-3 in the section labeled *To customize a paragraph, page, or column border* to open a Customize Border dialog box.

2 Choose **S**pacing. The Border Spacing dialog box appears.

3 Choose **A**utomatic Spacing to toggle this option off.

4 Choose **I**nside Spacing and enter numeric values in the text boxes adjacent to the Left, Right, Top, and Bottom items.

5 Choose Ou**t**side Spacing and enter numeric values in the text boxes adjacent to the Top and Bottom items.

6 Choose OK, Close, and OK to close the dialog boxes, activate the new line spacing, and return the program to the document's editing window. Alternatively, close all the dialog boxes by pressing Home, F7.

To add a shadow to the border

1 Follow steps 1-3 in the section labeled *To customize a paragraph, page, or column border* to open a Customize Border dialog box.

2 Choose S**h**adow. The Shadow dialog box appears.

3 Choose Shadow **T**ype and a shadow position: **N**one, **U**pper Left, **L**ower Left, U**p**per Right, or L**o**wer Right.

4 Choose Shadow **C**olor. The Color Selection dialog box appears. Follow steps 4-7 in the section labeled *To change the color of a border* to choose and adjust the color hue.

5 Choose the new color by double-clicking its name. Alternatively, choose **S**elect or Close.

6 Choose Shadow **W**idth and enter a numeric value in its text box.

7 Choose OK, Close, and OK to close the dialog boxes, activate the new shadowing, and return to the document's editing window. Alternatively, close all the dialog boxes by pressing Home, F7.

Fill Styles

Enhances a document with patterns and colors inside a border.

To set up Fill Styles

1 Follow steps 1-3 in the section labeled *To customize a paragraph, page, or column border* to open a Customize Border dialog box.

2 Choose **F**ill Style. The program displays the Fill Styles dialog box that includes a list box with fill style options.

3 Using the keyboard or mouse, move the highlight bar to the fill style you want. If you want to create your own fill style, choose **C**reate to open the New Fill Style Name dialog box.

4 Enter a name for the new fill style. Choose OK or press Enter. The Create Fill Style dialog box appears.

5 Choose Fill **T**ype. The program displays a pop-up scroll list with two options: **P**attern (the default) or **G**radient.

6 You also can access the following options from the Create Fill Style dialog box:

- Choose Fill **P**attern and the program displays the Predefined Patterns dialog box that offers 32 predefined fill patterns.

- Choose **C**olor... (Foreground) and the program displays the Color Selection dialog box. Follow steps 4-7 in the section labeled *To change the color of a border* to choose and adjust the color hue.

- Choose Color... (Background) and the program displays the Color Selection dialog box. Follow steps 4-7 in the section labeled *To change the color of a border* to choose and adjust the color hue.

7 Choose OK, Close, and OK to close the dialog boxes, activate the new fill style, and return the program to the document's editing window. Alternatively, close all the dialog boxes by pressing Home, F7.

To view the gradient fill in a document, choose **F**ile; or press Shift+F7. Then choose Print Preview.

Bullets

Enables you to create bulleted lists to display text in a manner that attracts the reader's attention.

To create bullets

1 Move the cursor to the beginning of the line on which you want to place the bullet.

2 Choose **T**ools, **M**acro, **P**lay; or press Alt+F10. The Play Macro dialog box appears.

3 Type **bullet** in the Macro text box. Choose OK or press Enter. Alternatively, use the File Manager (F5) or QuickList (F6) to locate and insert the file's name, and press Enter.

Shortcut

Click the pop-up button (the down arrow to the right of the **M**acro text box) or press ↓ to display a scroll list of the four most recently played macros. If `bullet` is listed, double-click it to start the macro running. Alternatively, use the keyboard to highlight its name and press Enter.

4 The macro displays the Bullet Inserter dialog box. Choose **I**nsert Bullet. The macro inserts the medium dot created by the 4,0 WordPerfect Character, followed by a tab code.

Tip

If you want the program to use a different bullet character, choose **C**hange Bullet. The macro displays the Edit Bullet Character dialog box, which lists six other bullet types plus an option to define a custom bullet using the WordPerfect Characters feature. After you designate or create the new character, the macro displays the Bullet Inserter dialog box. Choose **I**nsert Bullet. The macro inserts the new bullet character followed by a tab code.

Headers and Footers

Enables you to place information such as chapter titles, dates, or your company's name on every page of a document. You can place two headers and two footers on each page. Headers appear at the top of the page, and footers appear at the bottom. Graphics also can be used as headers or footers.

To create a header or footer

1 Choose **Layout**; or press Shift+F8. Choose **H**eader/ Footer/Watermark. The Header/Footer/Watermark dialog box appears.

2 Choose **H**eaders, Header **A** or Header **B**. Alternatively, choose **F**ooters, Footer **A** or Footer **B**. Depending on the option you choose, the appropriate header or footer dialog box appears.

3 Choose a page option: **A**ll Pages, **E**ven Pages, or **O**dd Pages.

4 Choose **C**reate. An editing window opens.

5 Type the text for the header or footer. Most of WordPerfect's formatting features are accessible from the pull-down menus, function keys, and shortcut keys.

Tip

If you want to use a graphic for the header or footer, choose **G**raphics, **R**etrieve Image. Type the name of a graphics-image file or use the File Manager (F5) or QuickList (F6) to locate and insert the file's name. Depending on the method used to designate the graphics file, choose **S**elect or OK, or press Enter to close the dialog box and insert the image into the header or footer.

---

6 Press F7 to close the header or footer editing window, insert the header or footer into the document, and return to the document's editing window.

Note

Whenever the program is in a header or footer editing window that displays the message Press F7 when done, you also can click the message to exit the window.

Tip

WordPerfect's Page Mode displays the document's text with its substructures, such as headers and footers, in the main editing window. This capability enables you to edit the document's main text while viewing the substructures' relationship to the body text. Page Mode does not enable you to edit a substructure in the main editing window. You can edit substructures only in the same editing window used to create them. To use Page Mode, choose View, Page Mode; or press Ctrl+F3 and choose Page Mode.

Watermarks

Enables you to print a company logo, a clip art graphic, a drawing, or headline text behind the text of a document.

To create a watermark

1 Choose Layout; or press Shift+F8. Choose Header/Footer/Watermark. The Header/Footer/Watermark dialog box appears.

2 Choose Watermark, Watermark **A,** or Watermark **B**. The Watermark A or Watermark B dialog box appears.

3 Choose a page option: All Pages, Even Pages, or Odd Pages.

4 Choose Create. The watermark's editing window opens.

5 Choose Graphics, Retrieve Image. Type the name of a graphics-image file or use the File Manager (F5) or QuickList (F6) to locate and insert the file's name. Depending on the method used to designate the graphics file, choose Select or OK, or press Enter to close the dialog box and insert the image into the header or footer.

6 Press F7 to close the watermark's editing window, insert the watermark into the document, and return the program to the document's editing window.

Note

Whenever the program is in a watermark editing window that displays the message Press F7 when done, you also can click the message to exit the window.

Note

The only method for viewing the watermark on-screen is to use WordPerfect's Print Preview feature. To use this feature, choose File; or press Shift+F7. Then choose Print Preview.

Envelopes and Bar Codes

Enables you to merge names and addresses from a data file to an envelope form. Additionally, you can print postal bar codes on envelopes using WordPerfect. For more information about merging data using WordPerfect, see *Merge*.

Merged Envelopes

Creates printed envelopes with a return address and names and addresses taken from your form letter's data file.

To create a form file for the envelopes

1 Choose Tools, Merge, Define; or press Shift+F9.

2 Choose Form, and then choose OK until you return to the document.

3 Choose Layout, Envelope; or press Alt+F12. The Envelope dialog box opens.

4 If you want an envelope size different from the one displayed, choose **E**nvelope Size and choose an envelope type from the list.

5 Choose **R**eturn Address. Type your name and address, and then press F7 to exit the Return Address text box.

6 Choose **M**ailing Address.

7 Choose **T**ools, **M**erge, **D**efine; or press Shift+F9.

8 Choose **F**ield, type the name or number of the first field for the mailing address, and then press Enter.

You also can choose List Field Names (F5), specify the path and file name of the data file for the mailing list, and then choose OK. Then highlight the field name for the first field, and choose Select.

9 Add the remaining fields by repeating step 7 and using one of the two methods in step 8.

10 Press F7 to exit the Mailing Address text box.

11 Choose **I**nsert. You return to the document.

12 Save the file under a distinctive file name so that you can find it later.

To merge the envelope with the data file

1 Choose **T**ools, **M**erge, **R**un; or press Ctrl+F9. The Run Merge dialog box opens.

2 Type the path and file name of the form file, or select the form file by using the File List or QuickList.

3 Type the path and file name of the data file.

4 Choose **O**utput, and choose the desired destination for the merge.

5 Choose Merge.

6 If you merged to the document window, make sure that you save the merged file.

Bar Codes

Adds a Postnet bar code to the envelope form file that prints as you print the envelopes.

1 Create an envelope form file by following steps 1-11 in that procedure.

2 Choose **T**ools, **M**erge, **D**efine; or press Shift+F9. The Merge Codes (Form File) dialog box appears. Choose **M**erge Codes. The All Merge Codes dialog box appears.

3 Choose POSTNET(string), and then choose Select. The Parameter Entry dialog box appears for the POSTNET(string) merge code.

4 Choose OK to insert the POSTNET code and return to the document.

5 Put the cursor between the parentheses in the POSTNET code.

6 Choose **T**ools, **M**erge, **D**efine, or press Shift+F9. The Merge Codes (Form File) dialog box appears. Choose **F**ield. The Parameter Entry dialog box appears for FIELD(field).

7 Type the zip code field name or number, and choose OK. WordPerfect returns you to the document and inserts the zip code field within the parentheses of the POSTNET merge code.

8 Save the file.

See also *Labels* (*Merged Labels*).

Equation Editor

Enables you to create equations with mathematical and scientific symbols and characters that print as graphic images within the document.

To create an equation

1 Move the cursor to the location where you want the equation created in the document.

2 Choose **G**raphics; or press Alt+F9. Choose Graphics **B**oxes, **C**reate. The Create Graphics Box dialog box appears.

3 Choose Contents. The program displays a pop-up scroll list.

4 Choose Equation.

> ┌ **Shortcut** ─────────────────
> If the equation previously has been saved as a graphics file, choose Filename. The program displays the Retrieve File dialog box. Type the name of the file or use the File Manager (F5) or QuickList (F6) to locate and insert the file's name.

5 Choose Based on Box Style. The Graphics Box Style dialog box appears.

6 Using the keyboard or mouse, move the highlight bar to `Equation Box`. Choose it by double-clicking it, choosing Select, or pressing Enter.

7 Choose Create Equation. Alternatively, if you retrieved an existing equation graphics file, choose Edit Equation. The Equation Editor appears.

8 Type the text for the equation in the Type Equation Text text box.

> ┌ **Tip** ─────────────────
> If the equation previously has been saved as a file, choose File, Retrieve; or press Shift+F10. The program displays the Retrieve Document dialog box. Click the pop-up button (the down arrow to the right of the Filename text field) or press ↓ to display a scroll list of the four most recently accessed files. If the file you need is listed, double-click its name, or use the keyboard to highlight its name and press Enter. Other file retrieval options include typing the name of the file or using the File Manager (F5) or QuickList (F6) to locate and insert the file's name.

9 Insert symbols, commands, and expressions from the Equation Palette located on the right side of the editing window as needed. (See the following procedure for details.)

Tip

If the symbols you need aren't listed on the palette, choose **S**et to display a pop-up scroll list of palette options: Commands, Large, Symbols, Greek, Arrows, Sets, Other, and Functions.

---

10 Choose **V**iew, **R**edisplay; or press Ctrl+F3. The program displays the equation in the equation window above the Type Equation Text text box.

11 Choose **F**ile, **C**lose, or press F7, to exit the equation editing window.

12 Choose OK, or press Enter or F7. The program returns to the document's editing window and inserts the equation as an image in a graphics box.

To insert commands and symbols

1 In the equation-editing window, if the symbols you need aren't listed on the palette, press F5 twice to display a pop-up scroll list of palette options: Commands, Large, Symbols, Greek, Arrows, Sets, Other, and Functions.

2 Using the keyboard or mouse, move the highlight bar to the palette set you want to use. Choose it by double-clicking its name or pressing Enter.

3 In the palette, double-click the command or symbol to insert it. Alternatively, use the arrow keys to highlight the command or symbol and press Enter or choose Keyword or Symbol, as appropriate, to insert the command into the text editing window.

You also can type commands into the editing window using the keyboard.

Fax

Enables you to fax your finished document directly from WordPerfect without having to leave the program.

To enable the Fax feature

1 At the DOS prompt in the WordPerfect program directory (usually C:\WP60), type **install** and press Enter.

2 Give the appropriate responses to the dialog boxes until the program displays the WordPerfect 6 Installation dialog box. Choose **D**evice Files (Sound, Graphics, Fax, Printer).

3 Give the appropriate responses to the dialog boxes until the program displays the Install: Device dialog box. Choose **F**ax Files. The Fax Device Options dialog box appears.

4 Choose the option that describes the Fax device: **F**axBios Compatible, **I**ntel SatisFAXtion, or **C**lass I or Class II Fax Modem. The appropriate files are installed to the WordPerfect program directory, including FAXB.COM.

5 When the program displays the FaxDirect CAS Setup Utility Screen, press Enter to continue.

6 In the dialog boxes that appear, give the appropriate responses to define the FAX device.

7 Press F10 to save and exit.

To activate the Fax feature

1 Run the fax modem's software.

2 Run the FAXB.COM program that Install placed in the directory containing the WordPerfect 6 program files (usually C:\WP60).

3 Start WordPerfect.

To send a document by using the Fax Manual Dial option

1 Choose **F**ile, **P**rint/Fax; or press Shift+F7. Choose Fax Services. The program displays the Fax Services: WordPerfect Corp. dialog box.

> **Note**
>
> If the Fax Services option is unavailable (grayed out), verify that the fax modem's software and FAXB.COM are correctly installed. If they are, check that the fax modem is correctly configured by sending a document outside of WordPerfect with it. If the fax modem transmits the document, contact WordPerfect technical support.

2 Choose **M**anual Dial. The program displays the Manual Dial dialog box.

3 Choose **R**ecipient, and type the name of the person, company, agency, or organization to whom the fax will be sent. Press Enter.

4 In the Fax # to Dial text box, enter the recipient's fax telephone number.

5 Choose OK or press Enter. The program displays the Send Fax dialog box.

6 Choose the option that tells WordPerfect where to find the document to be sent by the Fax feature: **F**ull Document, **P**age, **D**ocument on Disk, **M**ultiple Pages, **B**locked Text, or F**a**x on Disk.

The options for **D**ocument on Disk, **M**ultiple Pages, and F**a**x on Disk display dialog boxes that require additional information defining the document to be sent. The **B**locked Text option is available only if you use the Block feature to highlight a section of text in the document's editing window prior to accessing the Fax feature. (See also *Select.*)

Tip

If you want to save the document in the editing window for transmission at a later time, choose the Save as an Image for Fax on Disk option. The program places the cursor in the Filename text box for you to type a name for the file, which it saves as a fax graphic document.

7 Verify that the Coversheet option is marked as activated. If you want a high-quality rasterization (best-quality output), choose Resolution, Fine.

8 Choose Send Fax. The Fax feature automatically accesses the fax modem and transmits the document.

To create a Fax Phonebook entry

1 Choose File, Print/Fax; or press Shift+F7. Choose Fax Services. The program displays the Fax Services: WordPerfect Corp. dialog box.

2 Choose Phonebook. The program displays the Phonebook dialog box.

3 Choose Create Entry. The program displays the Create Entry dialog box.

4 Choose Name and enter the recipient's name in the text field.

5 Choose Fax Phone Number and enter the recipient's fax telephone number in its text field.

6 If you want to include an optional voice number, choose Voice Phone Number and enter the voice number in its text field.

7 Choose Destination Fax Machine. Choose all the rasterization options that the recipient's fax machine supports: Standard Resolution (a default), Fine Resolution (a default), 300 DPI Resolution, 400 DPI Resolution, and Binary File Transfer (BFT).

8 Choose OK. The program returns to the Phonebook dialog box and adds the new entry to its Phonebook Entries list. You can use the **E**dit option to change the item's information and the **D**elete option to remove the item when it is no longer needed.

9 Choose Close. The program returns to the Fax Services dialog box.

To send a document by using the Fax Phonebook option

1 Choose **F**ile, **P**rint/Fax; or press Shift+F7. Choose Fa**x** Services. The program displays the Fax Services: WordPerfect Corp. dialog box.

Note

If the Fax Services option is unavailable (grayed out), verify that the fax modem's software and FAXB.COM are correctly installed. If they are, check that the fax modem is correctly configured by sending a document outside of WordPerfect with it. If the fax modem transmits the document, contact WordPerfect technical support.

2 Using the keyboard or mouse, move the highlight bar to the Phonebook entry you want the Fax feature to use in transmitting the document.

3 Choose the entry by double-clicking its name or pressing Enter.

4 Choose **S**end Fax. The program displays the Send Fax dialog box.

5 Choose the option that tells WordPerfect where to find the document to be sent by the Fax feature: **F**ull Document, **P**age, **D**ocument on Disk, **M**ultiple Pages, **B**locked Text, or F**a**x on Disk.

The options for **D**ocument on Disk, **M**ultiple Pages, and F**a**x on Disk display dialog boxes that require additional information that defines the document to be sent. The **B**locked Text option is available only if you use the Block feature to highlight a section of text in the document's editing window prior to accessing the Fax feature. (See also *Select*.)

> ## Tip
>
> If you want to save the document in the
> editing window for transmission at a later
> time, choose the Save as an Image for Fax
> on Disk option. The program places the
> cursor in the Filename text box for you to
> type a name for the file, which it saves as a
> fax graphic document.

6 Verify that the Coversheet option is marked as
activated. If you want a high-quality rasterization
(best-quality output), choose Resolution, Fine.

7 Choose Send Fax. The Fax feature automatically
accesses the fax modem and transmits the
document.

File Manager

Shows drive and directory structure and contents and
handles file maintenance tasks. The File Manager also
enables you to change drives and directories, set up a
QuickList or Files List, or view the contents of a selected
file in the File View window. File Manager enables you to
open, retrieve, copy, move, delete, and save files.

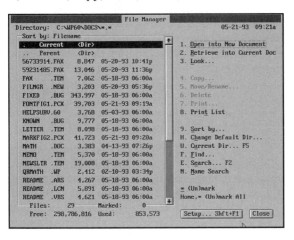

To set up the File Manager

1 Choose File, File Manager; or press F5. The Specify File Manager List dialog box appears.

2 Choose OK or press Enter. The program displays the File Manager dialog box, which contains the list of files in the default directory.

3 Choose Setup (Shift+F1). The program displays the File Manager Setup dialog box.

4 Choose Sort List By and designate one of the sorting options: Filename (the default), Extension, Date/Time, Size, Descriptive Name, Descriptive Type, or No Sort.

┌─ **Note** ──────────────────────────────┐

The Descriptive Name and Descriptive Type options are available only if Display List Mode, Descriptive Names and Types is active.

└──────────────────────────────────────┘

Choosing Filename, for example, tells the program to arrange the files alphabetically, and Date/Time arranges files by creation date, with the most recently created files listed first if you choose Descending Sort. If two or more files share the same creation date, they are secondarily sorted by creation time. Choosing Descriptive Type provides an alphabetical list of files by their descriptive names.

5 Choose Compressed Print for List to make the Print List option in the File Manager dialog box use a small font for printing out the directory list.

6 Choose OK or press Enter to save the settings and return to the File Manager dialog box. Alternatively, choose Cancel or press Esc to abandon the new settings.

To use the File Manager

1 Choose File, File Manager; or press F5. The Specify File Manager List dialog box appears.

2 Choose OK or press Enter to display the File Manager dialog box with the list of files in the default directory.

Alternatively, type the name of a different directory in the Directory text box to view the contents of that directory. Press = and the program displays the Change Default Directory dialog box, from which you can enter the name of a directory that the program temporarily uses as the default directory.

Alternatively, use QuickList (F6) or the Directory Tree (F8) to locate and display the files in a different directory.

3 Using the keyboard or the mouse, highlight a file in the Sort By list.

Shortcut

Choose **N**ame Search. The program displays the Name Search text box at the bottom of the screen. Type the first character in the file's name and the highlight bar moves to the first file that matches it. Beginning the text string with a \ limits the search to subdirectory names. Press the space bar to terminate the search operation when the bar highlights the file you want. Alternatively, choose **S**earch or press F2 to display the Search for Filename dialog box, which can search, filter, and display only files that match specific criteria.

4 Choose an option listed at the right of the dialog box: **O**pen into New Document, **R**etrieve into Current Document, **L**ook, **C**opy, **M**ove/Rename, **D**elete, or **P**rint. Alternatively, choose Close or press Esc to return to the document editing window without retrieving or opening a file.

Tip

Choose Print List to send the current file list to the printer.

To create a new directory by using File Manager

1 Choose File, File Manager; or press F5. The Specify File Manager List dialog box appears.

2 Choose OK or press Enter. The program displays the File Manager dialog box.

3 Choose Change Default Directory. The program displays the Change Default Directory dialog box.

4 Type the path name of the new directory.

Shortcut

Use QuickList (F6) or the Directory Tree (F8) to locate and insert the path name. Add the name of the new directory to the end of the path.

---

5 Press Enter. Choose Yes when the program displays the dialog box requesting confirmation to create the new directory. Choose No or press Esc to terminate the directory creation operation.

6 WordPerfect creates the directory but does not change to it. After the program redisplays the file list of the original directory, choose Close or press Esc to return to the document editing window.

To copy a file using the File Manager

1 Choose File, File Manager; or press F5. The Specify File Manager List dialog box appears.

2 Choose OK or press Enter. The program displays the File Manager dialog box.

3 Using the keyboard or the mouse, highlight a file in the Sort By list.

4 Choose Copy. The program displays the Copy dialog box.

5 In the Copy Highlighted File To text box, type the path name to the directory where you want the file copied.

Shortcut

Use QuickList (F6) or the Directory Tree (F8) to locate and insert the path name to the directory.

6 Choose OK or press Enter to start the copy operation. Alternatively, choose Cancel or press Esc to terminate the copy operation.

7 Choose Close or press Esc to return to the document editing window.

To delete a file by using the File Manager

1 Follow steps 1-3 in the instructions labeled *To copy a file by using the File Manager*, earlier in this section.

2 Choose **D**elete or press Del.

3 Choose **Y**es when the program displays the dialog box requesting confirmation to delete the file. Choose **N**o or press Esc to terminate the delete operation.

4 Choose Close or press Esc to return to the document editing window.

To use Redo with the File Manager

1 Choose **F**ile, **F**ile Manager; or press F5. The Specify File Manager List dialog box appears.

2 Choose Redo (F5) to redisplay the last directory viewed using File Manager during the current editing session, even if it is not the active default directory. The file list appears in the same state in which it appeared at the time you closed File Manager. (This feature does not work if the last directory viewed was on a floppy disk drive.)

3 Choose Close or press Esc to return to the document editing window.

QuickList

Lists the most frequently accessed directories and files for fast access.

To create the QuickList

1 Choose File, File Manager; or press F5. The Specify File Manager List dialog box appears.

2 Choose QuickList (F6). The program displays the QuickList dialog box.

3 Choose Create. The program displays the Create QuickList Entry dialog box.

4 The program defaults to choosing Description. Type a descriptive name for the directory in its text box.

5 Type a full path name and, optionally, a file mask in the Filename/Directory text box to add a new directory to the QuickList.

> **Shortcut**
>
> Use Directory Tree (F8) to locate and insert the path name to the directory.

The file mask can be a specific file name or a partial name with wild cards. WordPerfect displays only files matching the file mask when you use the QuickList feature. A path name and file mask such as C:\LETTERS*.JAN, for example, tells File Manager to display only those files in the C:\LETTER directory that have the extension JAN in their names.

6 Choose OK or press Enter to add the directory or file to the QuickList. Choose Cancel or press Esc to abandon the QuickList definition operation.

7 Repeat steps 3-6 until all new items are added.

8 Choose OK or press Enter to return to the QuickList dialog box. The additional directories are now listed in the QuickList dialog box.

9 Choose Close or press Esc to return to the document editing window.

To edit the QuickList

1 Choose File, File Manager; or press F5. The Specify File Manager List dialog box appears.

2 Choose QuickList (F6). The program displays the QuickList dialog box.

3 Choose Edit. The program displays the Edit QuickList Entry dialog box.

4 Type new information in the Description and Filename/Directory text boxes.

5 Choose OK or press Enter to return to the QuickList dialog box. The additional directories are now listed in the QuickList dialog box.

6 Choose Close or press Esc to return to the document editing window.

To use QuickList for file maintenance

1 Choose File, File Manager; or press F5. The Specify File Manager List dialog box appears.

2 Choose QuickList (F6). The program displays the QuickList dialog box.

3 Using the keyboard or the mouse, highlight the name or the descriptive name of the directory with which you want to work.

4 Double-click the name, choose Select, or press Enter. The File Manager dialog box appears, displaying the list of files for that directory. All the File Manager's options for copying, moving, renaming, and deleting are available for performing file maintenance operations.

5 Choose Close or press Esc to return to the document editing window.

To automatically update the QuickList

1 Choose File, Setup; or press Shift+F1. The program displays the Setup dialog box.

2 Choose Location of Files. The program displays the Location of Files dialog box.

3 Select the Update QuickList check box.

4 Choose OK, Close; or press Enter twice. Alternatively, press Home, F7 from the Location of Files dialog box. The program returns to the document editing window.

QuickFinder

Enables fast file indexing and searching to save you time.

To create QuickFinder indexes

1 Choose File, File Manager; or press F5. The Specify File Manager List dialog box appears.

2 Choose Use QuickFinder (F4). The program displays the QuickFinder File Indexer dialog box.

3 Choose Setup (Shift+F1). The program displays the QuickFinder File Indexes Setup dialog box.

4 Choose one of the List Indexes options: Personal (the default) or Shared.

5 Choose Location of Files. The program displays the QuickFinder Index Files dialog box.

6 As appropriate, choose either Personal Path or Shared Path and type the path and directory information for either the personal file directory or the shared file directory.

7 Choose OK or press Enter. The program returns to the QuickFinder File Indexes Setup dialog box.

If WordPerfect cannot find a directory by the name you entered in step 6, the program displays a dialog box asking for permission to create the directory. Choose Yes to create the new directory. Choose No to abandon the operation.

8 Choose Create Index Definition. The program displays the Create Index Definition dialog box and places the cursor in the Index Description text box.

9 Type a descriptive name for the index, and press Enter.

10 Press Enter. The cursor moves to the Index Filename text box and offers the first eight characters (without spaces) of the descriptive name as the default file name for the index.

11 Press Enter to accept the default. Alternatively, type a new name and press Enter. Either method redisplays the Create Index Definition dialog box.

12 Choose Add. The program displays the Add QuickFinder Index Directory Pattern dialog box.

13 Type a directory or file mask in the text box adjacent to Filename Pattern. You can use wild cards.

Shortcut

Use File List (F5) or QuickList (F6) to locate and insert the path name to the directory.

---

14 Choose Include Subdirectories to index files in all subdirectories of the directory specified in step 13. (The default is not to include subdirectories.)

15 Choose OK or press Enter. The program redisplays the QuickFinder File Indexes Setup dialog box.

16 Using the keyboard or the mouse, highlight the descriptive name of the directory for which you want to create a file index. If you want to create indexes for several directories, mark each item by pressing the asterisk key or the space bar.

17 Choose Generate. WordPerfect switches to DOS, creates the marked indexes, and the QuickFinder File Indexes Setup dialog box reappears.

18 Choose Close or press Enter to return to the QuickFinder File Indexer dialog box.

19 Choose OK or press Enter to return to the document.

To search indexes

1 Choose File, File Manager; or press F5. The Specify File Manager List dialog box appears.

2 Choose Use QuickFinder (F4). The program displays the QuickFinder File Indexer dialog box.

3 Choose Index and type the name of the index to search in the text box adjacent to it.

Shortcut

Click the pop-up button (the down arrow to the right of the Index text field) or press ↓ to display a scroll list of the four most recently accessed files. If the index you need is listed, double-click its name, or use the keyboard to highlight its name and press Enter.

4 Choose Word Pattern. Type the pattern for which you want to search in the text box.

Tip

Choose Operators (F5) to display a pop-up scroll list of search operators you can use in the word pattern. Use the keyboard or mouse to highlight an operator on the list. Double-click an operator, choose Insert, or press Enter. The operator appears in the Word Pattern text box.

5 Choose OK or press Enter to find files that contain the word pattern. The program displays a modified version of the File Manager dialog box with a list of the files containing the word pattern. You can use any of the File Manager's options to view, search, open, retrieve, rename, move, copy, print, or delete any file on the list.

6 If you do not use an option to open or retrieve a file, choose Close or press Enter. The program returns to the document editing window.

Fonts

Enables you to choose different typeface styles and appearance attributes to increase the visual appeal of your document. In addition to your printer's built-in fonts, you can choose among the graphics fonts that come with WordPerfect 6 or use TrueType fonts if Windows 3.1 is installed.

Using Fonts and Font Attributes

When you create a new document, WordPerfect 6 uses the initial font setting to choose the basic typeface that formats all text in the document's main body and substructures—page numbers, footnotes, headers, and so on.

However, you can use different fonts and font attributes in the same document or even on the same line with consecutive characters. An *initial font* controls the appearance of all text in a document, including substructures such as page numbering, footnotes, headers, and so on. A *base font*, however, overrides the initial font and formats body text from its location to the end of the document, unless another base font is inserted later in the document.

WordPerfect offers many options that enable you to temporarily or permanently override the initial font's text formatting. For example, you can do the following:

- Change the initial font for all documents or just the current document.

- Use a base font to override the initial font for some or all of the document's text.

- Use size/position attributes (small, large, subscript, and so on) to make a character or block of text smaller or larger.

- Use appearance attributes (bold, italics, redline, and so on) to emphasize important text.

To choose an initial font for all documents

1 Choose Layout; or press Ctrl+F8. Then choose Document, Initial Font. The program displays the Initial Font dialog box.

2 Choose All New Documents (Created with Current Printer). The option button next to this item darkens to show that it is active.

3 Choose Font or click the pop-up button adjacent to it. The program displays a pop-up scroll list of all available fonts. The currently active initial font is marked by the highlight bar and an asterisk.

4 Using the keyboard or mouse, move the highlight bar to the font you want to be the default for all new documents created with the current printer definition.

5 Choose the new font by double-clicking its name or pressing Enter.

6 Choose Size. The program highlights the current font size. Type a numeric value and press Enter.

Tip

Clicking the pop-up button adjacent to the Size option's text field displays a pop-up scroll list of font sizes. Double-click a value to choose it.

---

7 Choose OK twice to close the dialog box and save the new initial font setting. (If you accessed the Font feature by using Shift+F8 in step 1, you also must choose Close. Alternatively, exit the Initial Font dialog box by pressing Home, F7.)

To choose an initial font for the current document only

1 Choose Font, Font; or press Ctrl+F8. The program displays the Font dialog box.

2 Choose Setup (Shift+F1). The program displays the Font Setup dialog box.

3 Choose Select Initial Font. The program displays the Initial Font dialog box.

4 Choose Current Document Only (Text, Headers, and so on). The option button next to this item darkens to show that it is active.

5 Choose Font or click the pop-up button adjacent to it. The program displays a pop-up scroll list of all available fonts. The currently active initial font is marked by the highlight bar and an asterisk.

6 Using the keyboard or mouse, move the highlight bar to the font you want used as the default for all text and substructures in the current document.

7 Choose the new font by double-clicking its name or pressing Enter.

8 Choose Size. The program highlights the current font size. Type a numeric value and press Enter.

> **Tip**
>
> Clicking the pop-up button adjacent to the Size option's text field displays a pop-up scroll list of font sizes. Double-click a value to choose it.

9 Choose OK twice to close the dialog box and save the new initial font setting. (If you accessed the Font feature by using Ctrl+F8 in step 1, you also must choose Close. Alternatively, exit the Initial Font dialog box by pressing Home, F7.)

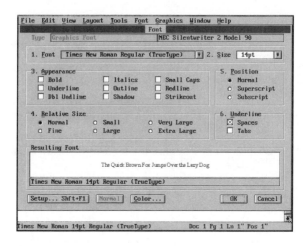

To change fonts temporarily

1 Choose Font, Font, or press Ctrl+F8. The Font dialog box appears.

2 Choose Font to display a drop-down list of fonts. The program displays a pop-up scroll list of all available fonts. The currently active initial font is marked by the highlight bar and an asterisk.

> ## Tip
>
> The program displays a sample of the font in the Resulting Font window near the bottom of the Font dialog box.

3 Using the keyboard or mouse, move the highlight bar to the font you want to be the default for all text and substructures in the current document.

4 Choose the new font by double-clicking its name or pressing Enter.

5 Choose Size. The program highlights the current font size. Type a numeric value and press Enter.

> ┌ **Tip** ─────────────────────────────
>
> Clicking the pop-up button adjacent to the
> Size option's text field displays a pop-up
> scroll list of font sizes. Double-click a value
> to choose it.

6 Choose OK twice to close the dialog box and save
the new initial font setting. (If you accessed the Font
feature by using Ctrl+F8 in step 1, you also must
choose Close. Alternatively, exit the Initial Font
dialog box by pressing Home, F7.)

To change fonts by using the Ribbon

1 Click the pop-up button adjacent to the name of the
active font at the right side of the Ribbon. The program displays a pop-up scroll list of all available
fonts.

2 Using the mouse or the keyboard, highlight the
font you need. Double-click it, or press Enter to
choose it.

> ┌ **Tip** ─────────────────────────────
>
> Hold down the mouse button and scroll the
> font list. When the bar highlights the font
> you need, release the mouse button.

3 Click the Point Size button. The program displays a
pop-up scroll list of sizes.

4 Hold down the left mouse button as you drag down
the list to highlight the size you want. Release the
mouse button.

To change the relative size or position of a font

1 Move the cursor to the location where you want to
change the font's relative size or position.

2 Use the Block feature to highlight the section of text.

3 Choose Font, Size/Position. The program displays a
pop-up menu with the following size and position
options: Normal Size, Fine, Small, Large, Very Large,

Extra Large, Normal Position, Subscript, or Super-script.

Alternatively, Press Ctrl+F8. The program displays the Font dialog box. Choose Relative Size and then a size option: Normal, Fine, Small, Large, Very Large, and Extra Large. Alternatively, choose Position from the Font dialog box and then choose a position option: Normal, Superscript, or Subscript.

Shortcut

If you want to apply more than one font attribute to a text block, use Ctrl+F8 to dis-play the Font dialog box. Unlike pull-down menu options, the Font dialog box enables you to apply several font attributes to the text block at one time. After you choose an attribute from the pull-down menus, the menu closes and the program turns off the highlighting. You must reblock the text for each attribute—a time-consuming proce-dure under the best of circumstances.

To change the size of a font

1 Move the cursor to the location where you want to change the font's size.

2 Choose Font, Font; or press Ctrl+F8. The Font dialog box appears.

3 Choose Size. The program highlights the current font size. Type a numeric value and press Enter.

Tip

Clicking the pop-up button adjacent to the Size option's text box displays a pop-up scroll list of font sizes. Double-click a value to choose it.

---

4 Choose OK twice to close the dialog box and save the new initial font setting. (If you accessed the Font feature by using Ctrl+F8 in step 2, you also must choose Close. Alternatively, exit the Initial Font dialog box by pressing Home, F7.)

Installing Soft Fonts

Soft fonts offer a wide variety of fonts and typefaces for enhancing documents. WordPerfect comes with a sampling of Adobe Type 1 fonts and Bitstream Speedo fonts. WordPerfect also offers internal support for the following types of fonts: TrueType, AutoFont, CG Intellifont, and HP LaserJet (bitmapped fonts).

WordPerfect uses its auxiliary Font Installer utility program to install these fonts into the WP.DRS file.

To designate the directories with soft fonts

1 Choose File, Setup; or press Shift+F1. Choose Location of Files.

2 Choose Graphics Font Data Files. If the path name information is correct, choose OK. Otherwise, continue with step 3.

3 Choose the font type that needs its path information corrected. Choose Edit Path.

4 Type the path to the directory containing the fonts.

5 Repeat as necessary steps 3 and 4 for the other font types.

6 Choose OK and Close.

To install the soft fonts

1 Choose Font, Font; or press Ctrl+F8. Choose Setup (Shift+F1).

2 Choose Install Fonts.

3 Choose a font type.

4 Mark each font you want to install by typing an asterisk (*) or by pressing the space bar. Repeat this step for each font you want installed.

5 Choose Install Marked Fonts.

6 Choose Continue if you need to install another font type. Otherwise, choose Exit.

7 Choose OK twice.

To add soft fonts

1 Choose Font, Font; or press Ctrl+F8. Choose Setup (Shift+F1).

2 Choose Select Cartridges/Fonts/Print Wheels.

3 Choose Soft Font from the Font Category list box.

4 Choose Quantity if you have upgraded printer memory. Enter the correct value and choose OK.

5 Choose Edit.

6 Choose the correct font group and press Enter.

7 Choose a font and type either a plus sign (+) or an asterisk (*). Fonts marked with an asterisk are present as a print job begins. Fonts marked with a plus sign can be loaded or unloaded during a job. Repeat this step for each font you want to install.

8 Choose OK.

9 Repeat steps 5 through 8 to add additional font groups.

10 Choose Close and then choose OK three times. Printer files are automatically updated with the selected fonts.

To add font cartridges or print wheels

1 Follow steps 1 through 4 in the *To add soft fonts* procedure.

2 Choose Edit and follow steps 7 through 10 in the procedure for adding soft fonts.

Footnotes and Endnotes

Serve as a reference to material found in the text. Used to cite sources or provide more detailed information.

Footnotes usually appear at the bottom of the page on which you find the footnote number. *Endnotes* are usually gathered together at the end of the document or at the ends of the chapters to which the notes refer.

Text is marked with a number to indicate a footnote or endnote for that text.

To create a footnote

1 Move the cursor immediately after the text that needs a footnote number.

2 Choose **Layout**; or press Ctrl+F7. Choose **Footnote, Create**.

3 Type the footnote text in the footnote editing window.

4 Press F7 to save the footnote. The program returns to the document's editing window.

To edit a footnote

1 Choose **Layout**; or press Ctrl+F7. Choose **Footnote, Edit**.

2 Type the footnote number to edit.

3 Choose OK or press Enter.

4 Edit the text of the footnote in the editing window.

5 Press F7 to save the changes. The program returns to the document's editing window.

To use footnote options

1 Move the cursor in front of the footnote for which you want to change options.

2 Choose **Layout**; or press Ctrl+F7. Choose **Footnote, Options**.

3 As necessary, choose the options and type new specifications in the option's text box or toggle the options active or inactive.

4 Choose OK, or press Enter.

To create an endnote

1 Move the cursor to the location in the document where you need to create an endnote.

2 Choose **Layout**; or press Ctrl+F7. Choose **Endnote, Create**.

3 Type text for the endnote in the editing window.

4 Press F7 to save the endnote. The program returns to the document's editing window.

To edit endnotes

1 Choose Layout; or Ctrl+F7. Choose Endnote, Edit.

2 Type the number of the endnote you want to edit.

3 Choose OK or press Enter.

4 Edit the text of the endnote in the editing window.

5 Press F7 to save the changes. The program returns to the document's editing window.

To use styles with footnotes or endnotes

1 Choose Layout, Styles; or press Alt+F8.

2 Choose Libraries Assigned to Document and type the location for Shared, Personal, or both.

3 Choose Options, List System Styles, and OK.

4 Highlight the Footnote or Endnote Style. Choose Edit.

5 Edit the style.

6 Copy the new style to your Personal Library.

See also *Styles*.

Tip

Font changes within a footnote or endnote control only that note. To change fonts in all footnotes or endnotes, edit the appropriate style.

Function Keys

Enables you to bypass the pull-down menu system and quickly access WordPerfect 6 features by pressing keys or key combinations.

The following table lists the key assignments for the new
WordPerfect 6 keyboard:

Key(s)	Feature Accessed
F1	Help
Shift+F1	Setup
Alt+F1	Writing Tools
Ctrl+F1	Shell
F2	Search Forward
Shift+F2	Search Backward
Alt+F2	Replace
Ctrl+F2	Speller
F3	Switch To
Shift+F3	Switch
Alt+F3	Reveal Codes
Ctrl+F3	Screen
F4	Indent
Shift+F4	Left-Right Indent
Alt+F4	Block
Ctrl+F4	Move
F5	File Manager
Shift+F5	Date
Alt+F5	Mark Text
Ctrl+F5	Outline
F6	Bold
Shift+F6	Center
Alt+F6	Flush Right

continues

Key(s)	Feature Accessed
Ctrl+F6	Tab Align
F7	Exit
Shift+F7	Print/Fax
Alt+F7	Columns/Tables
Ctrl+F7	Notes
F8	Underline
Shift+F8	Format
Alt+F8	Styles
Ctrl+F8	Font
F9	End Field
Shift+F9	Merge Codes
Alt+F9	Graphics
Ctrl+F9	Merge/Sort
F10	Save As
Shift+F10	Open/Retrieve
Alt+F10	Macro Play
Ctrl+F10	Record Macro
F11	Reveal Codes
Shift+F11	WP Characters
Alt+F11	Table Editor
Ctrl+F11	Tab Set
F12	Block
Shift+F12	Bookmark
Alt+F12	Envelope
Ctrl+F12	Save

Graphics

Offers powerful desktop publishing features by giving you the capability to mix text, typefaces, and graphics from a variety of sources.

To create a graphics box

1   Move the cursor to the location where you want the graphics box inserted.

2   Choose **G**raphics; or press Alt+F9. Choose Graphics **B**oxes, **C**reate.

3   Choose Based on Box St**y**le.

4   Highlight a box style. Choose **S**elect.

5   Choose Close and OK. The program returns to the document's editing window.

To retrieve a graphics image from disk

1   Move the cursor to the location where you want the graphic inserted.

2   Choose **G**raphics; or press Alt+F9. Choose **R**etrieve Image.

3   Type the path and file name. Choose OK or press Enter; or choose File List (F5) or QuickList (F6) to find and open the file.

4   Click and drag the graphics image to reposition it; or choose **G**raphics; or press Alt+F9. Choose Graphic **B**oxes, **E**dit, Document Box **N**umber.

5   Type the figure's number, and choose **E**dit Box.

6   From the Edit Graphics dialog box, choose the appropriate options to edit the figure's size and position. Choose OK or press Enter to save changes.

Image Editor

Enables you to edit graphics images, with options for cropping, scaling, rotating, adjusting position, selecting brightness and contrast, changing the size, and so on.

To use the Image Editor

1 Create a graphics box and retrieve an image into it as described in the preceding two sections.

2 In the Create Graphics Box dialog box, choose Image Editor.

3 Choose the options you need from the Button Bar, the menu bar, and the mnemonic list at the bottom of the dialog box. Type new settings in the text boxes next to these options.

4 Choose File, Close (or press F7) to exit the Image Editor.

5 Choose OK. The program returns to the document's editing window.

Graphics Lines

Creates vertical and horizontal lines in a document.

To create graphics lines

1 Move the cursor to the location where you need the line inserted.

2 Choose **G**raphics; or press Alt+F9. Choose Graphics Lines, **C**reate.

3 Choose Line **O**rientation and **H**orizontal or **V**ertical. (The default is **H**orizontal.)

4 Use the other options as necessary to define the line.

5 Choose OK or press Enter. The program returns to the document's editing window, where it inserts the line.

To edit graphics lines by using the mouse

1 Double-click the line and drag it to a new location.

2 Click the line and drag one of its *handles* (the little black boxes that appear around the line) to increase or decrease the thickness of the line.

To edit graphics lines by using the keyboard

1 Choose **G**raphics; or press Alt+F9. Choose Graphics Lines, **E**dit.

2 Choose Graphics Line **N**umber. Type the number of the line to be edited.

> **Tip**
>
> You can choose Next Graphics Line or Previous Graphics Line to find the line to edit.

3 Choose **E**dit Line.

4 Choose the options you need to change.

5 Choose OK or press Enter. The program saves the changes and returns to the document's editing window.

Horizontal positioning options do the following:

Position	Result
Left or Right	Positions line against either margin.
Center	Centers line between margins.
Full	Draws the line from the left edge to the right edge across the page.
Specify	Sets the distance from the top edge of the page and the line position in relation to the top edge of the page.

Vertical positioning options do the following:

Position	Result
Top	Draws the line from the top of the page to the cursor.

continues

Position	Result
Bottom	Draws the line from the bottom of the page to the cursor.
Left Margin	Positions the line to the left of the left margin.
Right Margin	Positions the line to the right of the right margin.
Between Columns	Positions the line to the right of the column number that you enter in the text box.
Set	Enables you to position the line a specified distance from the left edge of the page.
Specify	Sets the distance from the left edge of the page to the beginning of the line and in relation to the left edge of the page.

Help

Provides on-line context-sensitive help for features accessed while working in a document. Using Help's Coaches and Tutorials facilitates learning both basic and advanced WordPerfect 6 functions.

Help is divided into the following sections:

- *Contents* is a menu of the available Help functions.

- *Index*, with the *Name Search* feature, enables you to search for any topic.

- *How Do I* describes specific procedures.

- *Glossary* uses definitions to explain terms. (Hold the mouse button on any term to read the definition, or place the cursor on the term and choose Look.)

- *Coaches* leads you through the steps for performing certain tasks while creating/editing a document.

- *Macros* is an on-line Macros manual to help you learn about the Macro feature.

- *Tutorial* shows how to perform certain tasks by providing practice lessons.

- *WP Info* provides information about your copy of WordPerfect 6, your registration number, network, memory, and current printer.

- *Keyboard* lists the keystrokes used for accessing program features.

- *Template* lists the function key assignments.

- *Shortcut Keys* describes handy shortcut keystrokes for common tasks.

You can access Help in one of the following ways:

- Choose **H**elp in the menu bar.

- Press F1.

To access Help

1 Choose **H**elp; or press F1.

2 Choose an option from the **H**elp menu.

Shortcut

Use **N**ame Search to find a topic in a hurry. Choose **P**revious to jump back to the previous topic.

3 Highlight the topic you want to read.

4 Double-click the topic, or press Enter.

5 Choose Cancel to close Help.

To use How Do I

1 Choose **H**elp; or press F1. Choose **H**ow Do I.

2 Highlight a topic, and double-click it or press Enter.

3 Choose Cancel or press Esc to exit Help.

To use Coaches

1 Choose **Help**; or press F1. Choose C**o**aches.

2 Highlight a topic, and double-click it or press Enter.

3 Select the check box next to an item.

4 Choose Continue or press F7 to advance through the steps.

See also *Coaches*.

To use Tutorial

1 Choose **Help**; or press F1. Choose Tutorial.

2 Respond appropriately to the questions presented until the program displays the WordPerfect 6.0 Tutorial - Main Menu.

3 Choose a lesson by highlighting a topic and double-clicking it or pressing Enter.

4 Exit the Tutorial by clicking Exit Tutorial or pressing F7.

Hypertext

Enables you to link nonsequential portions of a document to other portions of the same document or to other documents, or to run a macro. This feature is useful for jumping from one Bookmark to another or for running a macro within a document.

To create a Hypertext Link

1 Block the text to use as a Hypertext button.

2 Choose **Tools**; or press Alt+F5. Choose **H**ypertext, C**r**eate Link.

3 Choose Go to **B**ookmark. Type the name of the bookmark, or choose List Bookmarks (F5) to insert a Bookmark name.

4 Choose Go to **O**ther Document and type the name of the other document.

5 Choose Bookmark to create a link that jumps to a Bookmark in another WordPerfect 6 document. Type the name of the Bookmark in the other document, or choose List Bookmarks (F5) to insert a bookmark name.

6 Choose Run **M**acro, and type the name of a WordPerfect 6 macro.

7 Choose **H**ighlighted Text to create a Hypertext button using enhanced text. Choose B**u**tton (Graphic) to create a Hypertext button using a WordPerfect graphics image. Buttons can be blank or can include text or graphics images. A button appears on-screen as a graphic image only in Graphics and Page Modes.

8 Choose OK or press Enter. The program returns to the document's editing window and inserts the Hypertext button.

To edit the Hypertext Style

1 Choose **T**ools; or press Alt+F5. Choose **H**ypertext, Edit Hypertext **S**tyle.

2 Edit the formatting codes. (The default settings are Bold and Underline.)

3 Choose or press F7.

4 Choose OK or press Enter. The program updates the Hypertext style and returns to the document's editing window.

To use Hypertext Jump/Run for a single jump/run

1 If a document contains Hypertext links but the Hypertext feature is inactive, move the cursor to a Hypertext link.

2 Choose **T**ools; or press Alt+F5. Choose **H**ypertext, **J**ump/Run.

To return from a jump

1 Choose **T**ools; or press Alt+F5.

2 Choose **H**ypertext, **R**eturn from Jump.

To activate Hypertext links

1 Choose **T**ools; or press Alt+F5. Choose **H**ypertext, Hypertext is **A**ctive.

2 Choose OK or press Enter. The program activates the document's Hypertext links and returns to the document's editing window.

If Hypertext is active, moving the cursor to a Hypertext button and clicking or pressing Enter does one of the following:

- Moves the cursor to the linked Bookmark.

- Moves the cursor to another document.

- Runs a macro.

If Hypertext is active, pressing Tab jumps to the next link and Shift+Tab jumps to the previous link.

Index

Creates an index for a document; automatically generates page number references.

WordPerfect offers two methods for creating an index. The hard way is to mark manually each word or phrase. The easy way is to create a *concordance file* that searches the document for each occurrence of the word or phrase and inserts the correct page numbers in the index. With either method, you also must define the location and numbering style, and generate the index.

To create and use a concordance file

1 Open a blank document.

2 Type an entry for the index and press Enter. Place only one index entry on each line. Repeat until all items are in the file.

3 Save the concordance file.

4 Define an index, as described in the procedure *To define an index* later in this section, including the name of the concordance file.

5 Generate the index automatically.

To create an index by using marked text

1 Move the cursor to the word you want in the index. If you want a phrase, block the words in it.

2 Choose Tools; or press Alt+F5. Choose Mark Text, Index.

3 Press Enter to accept the word or phrase as a heading. Type an optional subhead.

4 Choose OK or press Enter.

5 Repeat steps 1 through 4 to mark all other headings and subheadings to be included.

6 Define the index as described in the following procedure.

7 Generate the index, as described in the procedure *To generate an index*.

To define an index

1 Move the cursor to a blank page at the end of the document.

2 Press Ctrl+Enter to create a hard page break so that the index starts on a new page.

3 Type a title for the index. Press Enter several times to create blank lines between the title and the index.

4 Choose Tools; or press Alt+F5. Choose Define, Index.

5 Choose an option under Numbering Mode. The default is ...# Flush Right.

6 Choose Concordance Filename and type the file name.

7 Choose OK or press Enter. The program returns to the document's editing window.

8 Generate the index as described in the following procedure.

To generate an index

1 Choose Tools; or press Alt+F5. Choose **G**enerate (Tables, Indexes, Cross-References, and so on).

2 Choose OK or press Enter. The program returns to the document's editing window and creates the index.

Keyboard Definition

Enables you to change key assignments.

To select a keyboard definition

1 Choose File, Setup; or press Shift+F1. Choose **K**eyboard Layout.

2 Choose a keyboard file from the list box.

3 Choose **S**elect, Close. The program activates the keyboard definition and returns to the document's editing window.

To create a custom keyboard definition

1 Choose File, Setup; or press Shift+F1. Choose **K**eyboard Layout.

2 Select a keyboard definition in the list box to be used as a template for the new definition.

3 Choose **C**reate and type a name for the new keyboard definition.

4 Choose OK or press Enter.

5 Choose **C**reate, **K**ey. Press the key or key combination to be assigned an action.

6 Choose **D**escription and type a description of the key assignment.

7 Choose an option under Action Type: **T**ext, **C**ommand, or **M**acro.

If an action already is assigned to these keystrokes, the assignment appears in the text boxes. Choose another set of keystrokes to define.

8 If you chose **C**ommand in step 7, choose a command from the list box by highlighting the command and double-clicking it or pressing Enter.

If you chose **M**acro in step 7, choose Edit/Create Macro. Create the macro and press F7.

If you chose **T**ext in step 7, type the text you want assigned to the key definition.

9 After making all key assignments, choose OK.

10 Highlight the new definition and choose **S**elect. If you accessed the Keyboard feature by pressing Shift+F1 in step 1, choose Close. The program returns to the document's editing window.

Keyboard assignments remain active until you change them again.

Labels

Enables you to create mailing labels, disk labels, tickets for events, name badges, and so on. You can create the labels individually or use them with the Merge feature to produce a mass mailing.

To set up labels

1 Move the cursor to the location where the labels should begin.

2 Choose **L**ayout; or press Shift+F8. Choose **P**age, Labels.

3 Choose Display **L**aser, Display **T**ractor-Fed, or Display **B**oth, as appropriate for your printer.

4 Highlight a label type in the list box and choose it by double-clicking it or pressing Enter.

5 Choose options as necessary to define the labels.

6 Choose OK, Close, OK. The program returns to the document's editing window.

To type labels

1 Type each line and press Enter at the end of each line.

2 Choose **L**ayout; or press Shift+F8. Choose **P**age, Center Current Page.

3 Press Ctrl+End at the end of the label.

4 Press PgUp or PgDn to move the cursor from label to label, as necessary.

To edit a label definition

1 Choose **L**ayout; or press Shift+F8. Choose **P**age, Labels.

2 Highlight the label you want to modify, and choose **E**dit.

3 Change the Label **D**escription.

4 Choose the other options as necessary to edit the definition.

5 Choose OK and Close as necessary. The program saves the changes and returns to the document's editing window.

Merged Labels

Enables you to create labels for mass mailings easily.

To create merged labels

1 Create a data file containing the names and addresses for your mailing list. (You can use the same data file created to merge with form letters, as described under *Data Files* in the *Merge* section.)

2 Create a form file containing the field names for the mailing labels, as described in the following procedure.

To create a form file for labels

1 At the beginning of a new document, choose **L**ayout; or press Shift+F8. Choose **D**ocument Initial Codes.

2 Choose **L**ayout; or press Shift+F8. Choose **P**age, Labels.

3 Choose Center **P**ages and choose OK.

4 Choose **F**ont, **F**ont; or press Ctrl+F8. Choose **F**ont and pick a small monospaced or proportional font.

5 Choose OK and press F7 to exit.

6 Choose **T**ools, **M**erge, **D**efine **M**erge Codes; or press Shift+F9, Shift+F9. Insert the `Label` merge code, giving it a unique name.

7 Repeat step 6 to insert the first field name. Press the space bar and insert the second field name. Press Enter to end the line and go to the next one. Continue to insert field names for the rest of the label. Press Ctrl+Enter to go to the next label.

8 Repeat step 6 to insert the `Nextrecord` merge code in the second label.

9 Repeat step 6 to insert the `Go (label)` merge code, and repeat the name of the Label command.

10 Save the form file under a distinctive name.

If you have trouble fitting all the information you need into a label, try changing to a smaller font.

Print out a few test labels on plain paper to check for alignment of the print and of the label itself before printing a large number of labels. You may need to adjust the text or set different margins within the labels.

See also *Merge*.

List

Enables you to create a list of keywords or headings in your document.

To create a list

1 Block the text to mark for the first item.

2 Choose **T**ools, **L**ist, **M**ark; or press Alt+F5 and choose **L**ist.

3 Type in the dialog box all requested information, such as title, list number, numbering style, and so on. Choose OK.

4 Continue selecting and marking text for each item, and choose OK to add it to the list.

Now you must define the list.

To define a list

1 Choose Tools, List, Define; or press Alt+F5, Define, List.

2 Choose Create.

3 Fill in the requested information.

4 Choose OK.

To generate the list

1 Move the cursor to a separate page by pressing Ctrl+End to insert a hard page break.

2 On the new page, type the title of the list. Press Enter several times to insert blank lines between the title and the list.

3 Place the cursor where you want the list inserted.

4 Choose Tools; or press Alt+F5. Choose Generate and Yes. The list appears on the new page.

To delete an item from the list, open Reveal Codes by choosing View, Reveal Codes; or press F11 or Alt+F3. Move the cursor to the list marker by the item to be deleted. Press Del.

Indexes, tables of contents, tables of authorities, lists, and cross-references are all accessed from the Tools pull-down menu or by pressing Alt+F5.

Macros

Speeds up typing and format changes by enabling you to record a sequence of keystrokes that can be played back as needed. Macros automate time-consuming and tedious tasks.

Macros are special files that contain a sequence of commands to perform various functions. They can change formats and layouts, insert a complimentary close in a letter, change paper size, and so on. This feature saves many keystrokes and mouse clicks, enabling you to complete tasks much faster.

Making a Macro

Recording a macro requires pressing only a few keystrokes.

To record a macro

1 Choose **T**ools, **M**acro, **R**ecord; or press Ctrl+F10.

2 Type a file name for the macro, and press Enter.

3 Add formatting commands to the macro by choosing them from the menus.

4 Press Ctrl+PgUp to open the Macro Control dialog box, and then insert macro commands and variables from the list box.

5 To stop recording the macro, choose **T**ools, **M**acro, **S**top; or press Ctrl+F10.

To play back a macro

1 Choose **T**ools, **M**acro, **P**lay; or press Alt+F10.

2 Select from the file list the macro you want to play.

3 Choose OK, or press Enter.

Macro Compiler

Automatically records the macro whenever you record or play it. If errors are found, the compiler notifies you of these and then enables you to edit the macro.

To edit a macro during recording

1 Choose **T**ools, **M**acro, **R**ecord; or press Ctrl+F10.

2 Type a file name for the macro, and choose OK.

3 While editing a macro, you can press Shift+F3 to switch to another document window in which WordPerfect records the commands for you. Use Ctrl+PgUp to open the Macro Control dialog box, and then select the macro commands and variables you want.

You also can select WordPerfect commands from the menus. Press Shift+F3 again to return to the original macro. The commands you record in the other window are inserted in the macro where the cursor stopped.

4 Choose **T**ools, **M**acro, **S**top; or press Ctrl+F10.

Tip

The Help feature contains an on-line Macro Manual with more detailed information.

You can assign a macro to the Button Bar or to a keystroke combination on your keyboard.

See also *Button Bars* and *Keyboard Layout.*

Master Document

Organizes large writing projects into a fixed format used to generate indexes and tables of contents and provide automatic page numbering, while still enabling you to work on individual subdocuments in the project.

A *master document* is a special file that usually contains some text but primarily contains codes linking the master to all the subdocuments that go with it. The *subdocuments* are the sections of text that make up each chapter. If you are writing a book with many chapters, you can use the master document to organize your material and pull it together. A master document also is used to create a table of contents and index.

To use a master document

1 Create the subdocuments for the project and store them as individual files.

2 Create the master document and insert document links to show WordPerfect where the subdocuments are to be located within the master document, as described in the following procedure.

3 Expand the master document to pull in all the subdocuments, as described in step 6 of the following procedure.

4 Generate the index and table of contents.

5 Condense the master document, as described in the procedure following the next one, and store the subdocuments as separate files again.

To create the master document and insert document links

1 Start your master document on a clear screen.

2 Move the cursor to the location where you want to insert the link.

3 Choose File, Master Document, Subdocument; or press Alt+F3 and choose Master Document, Subdocument.

4 Type the file name, or select a file from the list. Choose OK.

5 Repeat steps 3 through 4 until all links are inserted.

Tip

If you want each subdocument to start on a fresh page, press Ctrl+Enter to insert a hard page break after each entry in the master document.

---

6 Expand the master document to pull in all the links by choosing File, Master Document, Expand; or press Alt+F5 and choose Master Document, Expand.

WordPerfect pulls all the subdocuments into the master document in the correct order.

Reminder

You must expand the master document before you can create and generate an index or table of contents.

Condensing a master document removes the subdocuments from the master document and stores them as separate files, but the links remain.

To condense a master document

1 Choose File, **M**aster Document, **C**ondense; or press Alt+F5 and choose **M**aster Document, **C**ondense.

2 Choose **S**ave Subdoc if you made changes in the expanded master document.

3 Choose OK.

See also *Index*, *Table of Contents*, *Table of Authorities*.

Math

Enables simple mathematical calculations in a document.

To turn math on

1 Move the cursor to the location where you want to start a math column.

2 Choose **T**ools, Math, **O**n; or press Alt+F7 and choose Math, Math **O**n.

To define a math column

1 Choose View, Reveal **C**odes; or press F11 or Alt+F3.

2 Move the cursor just after the [Math On] code in the document.

3 Choose **T**ools, Math, **D**efine; or press Alt+F7 and choose **M**ath, Math **D**efine.

4 Press the letter corresponding to the column you want to define. (Twenty-four columns are available, from A-X.)

5 Choose a Column Type. (See the following subsection for the available column types.) If you choose Calculation as the column type, type a formula in the Formula text box.

6 Choose how negative numbers are to appear. The default is to display them in parentheses. The other option is to display them with a minus sign (–) before the number.

7 Type the number of digits to be displayed after a decimal in the Digits After Decimal text box. The default is 2.

8 Choose OK or press Enter.

To calculate math

1 Make sure that the cursor is inside the math portion of the document.

2 Choose Tools, Math, Calculate; or press Alt+F7 and choose Math, Calculate.

To turn math off

Choose Tools, Math, Off; or press Alt+F7 and choose Math, Math On (this setting is a toggle).

Column Definition Options

Numeric columns enable you to add positive and negative numbers down a column to create subtotals, totals, and grand totals.

Calculation columns enable you to create a formula across columns by using numbers from the same row.

Total columns display totals from the column to the left.

Text columns enable you to include descriptions in row titles or labels in a column. Numbers in text columns are treated as text and do not calculate.

See also *Tables*.

Merge

Enables you to combine two files into one file, inserting variable data into a fixed format as you run the merge.

Merge is most commonly used to combine a form letter with a mailing address list. You first create a *data file* containing the names and addresses set up in fields and records.

These individual items (such as a first name) are known as *fields*. All the fields that belong together (such as the name and address of one person) make up one *record*. WordPerfect provides two types of data files: a text data file and a table data file. In a text data file, each field is marked by an [MRG:ENDFIELD] code and records are marked by an [MRG:ENDRECORD] code. In a table data file, columns represent fields and rows represent records.

You may have as many records as you have names on your address list (limited only by the amount of room on your disk drive). You may have up to 255 fields in each record in a text data file and 64 fields in each record in a table data file.

Each data record in a data file, however, must contain the same number of fields as all the other records in the file, even if you must leave one or more fields blank. Each field within a record must fall in the same order as in all other records.

See also *Envelopes and Bar Codes*.

Data File

Holds the information to be merged with a form file. An example of a data file is an address list for mass mailings.

To create a data (text) file

1 In a new document, choose **T**ools, **M**erge, **D**efine; or press Shift+F9. The Merge Codes dialog box appears. Choose **D**ata [Text] to define the current document as a text data file. The Merge Codes (Text Data File) dialog box appears. Choose OK to return to the document.

2 Type the information for the first field of the first
record in the data file document. For example, the
first field may be a title, such as **Mr.**, **Ms.**, or **Dr.**

3 Press F9 immediately after the information you
typed for the first field (after the period in a title,
for example). Do not leave a space. In your document, ENDFIELD appears at the end of the field, a
[MRG:ENDFIELD] code and [HRt] code are inserted,
the cursor moves to the next line, and Field: 2
appears on the status line at the bottom left of the
screen. This tells you WordPerfect is ready for you
to enter the information for the second field of the
record.

4 Continue typing the data for each of the fields of the
first record, pressing F9 at the end of each field.

For a form letter, you may want fields for title, first
name, last name, street address, city, state, and zip
code. Each field is numbered consecutively, and the
field number is incremented automatically each time
you press F9.

5 To end the record, press Shift+F9, **D**ata [Text].
In your document, ENDRECORD appears, a
[MRG:ENDRECORD] code and a [HPg] code are inserted, and the cursor is placed at the beginning
of the next record. Field: 1 appears on the status
line, telling you that WordPerfect is ready for you to
type the information for the first field of the next
record.

6 Continue typing records until your entire mailing list
is in the data file.

7 Save your data file under a distinctive name. For a
Christmas letter address list, for example, you may
choose XMAS.DTA.

To create a data (table) file

1 In a new document, choose **T**ools, **M**erge, **D**efine; or
press Shift+F9. The Merge Codes dialog box ap-
pears. Choose Data [**T**able] to define the current
document as a table data file. The Merge Codes
(Table Data File) dialog box appears.

2 Choose Create a Table with Field Names. The Field Names dialog box appears.

3 Type a name (for example, **title**) and choose OK for each field in the record. The field names appear in the Field Name List. After you have added field names, choose OK until you return to the document. A table is created with the field names listed at the top of each column. The cursor is placed in the first field of the first record.

4 Type the information for the first field of the first record in the data file document. For example, the first field may be a title, such as **Mr.**, **Ms.**, or **Dr.**

5 Press Tab to move the next field.

6 Continue typing the data for each of the fields of the first record, pressing Tab at the end of every field.

7 After you press Tab in the last cell of a row (which represents the last field of a record), a new row is added to the table, enabling you to enter another record.

8 Continue typing records until your entire mailing list is in the data file.

9 Save your data file under a distinctive name. For a Christmas letter address list, for example, you may choose XMAS.DTA.

Form File

Holds a form into which you want the data from the data file inserted. In the case of a mass mailing, this form file contains a form letter you want to send to each of the names in your address list.

Each of the field numbers in the form file corresponds to a field number in your data file. (You may prefer to name the fields so that they are easier to remember.)

To create a form file

1 In a new document, choose **T**ools, **M**erge, **D**efine; or press Shift+F9. The Merge Codes dialog box appears. Choose **F**orm to define the current document as a merge form. The Merge Codes (Form File) dialog box appears. Choose OK to return to the document.

2 Set up the format you want for your letter, including margins, line spacing, font, justification, and so on. This example assumes you are typing a form letter that you want to send to all the names in a data file.

3 Type any text, such as the date, that you want to appear before you insert the first field of a record.

4 Place the cursor where the name and address is to start.

5 Choose **T**ools, **M**erge, **D**efine; or press Shift+F9. Choose **F**orm to access the Parameter Entry dialog box for Field.

6 If you are using Field Names, type in this text box the name of the field you want to insert, and then choose OK. If you are using field numbers, type the number in the text box instead. You return to your document and WordPerfect inserts a code—for example, FIELD(title).

Choose List Field Names (F5) and, in the Select Data File For Field Names dialog box, type the data file name. The List Field Names dialog box appears, showing the defined field names.

7 Continue inserting fields at the appropriate places in your document by repeating steps 5 and 6 until you have entered all the fields. Add the correct spacing and punctuation where needed.

8 Type the text of the letter.

9 Save the letter under a distinctive file name. (Save a Christmas letter to clients, for example, under a file name such as XMAS.FRM.)

Merging Primary and Data Files

Now you must merge everything together before you can mail it.

To merge

1 Choose **T**ools, **M**erge, **R**un; or press Ctrl+F9, **M**erge. The Run Merge dialog box appears.

2 Type the names of your form and data files in the appropriate text boxes.

3 Choose Merge. The two files are merged on-screen.

4 Save your merged list under a distinctive name. (If your document is a Christmas greetings letter, for example, save it as XMAS.LTR.)

Merging to the Printer

If you are performing a very long merge, you may prefer to merge directly to the printer. To do so, you must insert Merge Codes at the end of your form file.

To merge to the printer

1 Choose **T**ools, **M**erge, **R**un; or press Ctrl+F9, **M**erge. The Run Merge dialog box appears.

2 Type the names of your form and data files in the appropriate text boxes.

3 Choose **O**utput, **P**rinter.

4 Choose Merge. The two files are merged, and the form with the merged data inserted is printed.

To insert merge codes to merge at the printer

1 Place the cursor on a blank line at the end of the form file.

2 Press Shift+F9, Shift+F9 to open the All Merge Codes dialog box.

3 Choose PAGEOFF from the list of codes in the dialog box, and choose **S**elect to insert the code in the form file and return to the document.

4 Repeat steps 2 and 3, but choose PRINT from the list of codes.

5 Save your file, and then run the merge. The PAGEOFF and PRINT codes send your merged letter to the printer.

The letters are printed with the names, addresses, and salutations you entered in your data file.

Merging Form Letters, Addresses, and Envelopes Simultaneously

The new envelope feature has the capability to generate envelopes while merging a form letter with the mailing list, and then to send the output directly to the printer.

To generate envelopes while merging

1 Create or open a form file for the letter.

2 Create a data file containing the mailing list names and addresses.

3 Choose Tools, Merge, Run; or press Ctrl+F9 and choose Merge. The Run Merge dialog box appears.

4 Type path and file name information for the letter form file and the data file in the appropriate text boxes in the Run Merge dialog box.

5 Choose Data File Options, and then choose Generate an Envelope for Each Data Record. The Envelope dialog box appears so that you can define the envelope.

6 If you want an envelope size different from the one displayed, choose Envelope Size and choose an envelope type from the list.

7 Choose Return Address. Type your name and address, and then press F7 to exit the Return Address text box.

8 Choose Mailing Address.

9 Choose Tools, Merge, Define; or press Shift+F9.

10 Choose Field, type the name or number of the first field for the mailing address, and then press Enter.

You also can choose List Field Names (F5), specify the path and file name of the data file for the mailing list, and then choose OK. Then highlight the field name for the first field, and choose Select.

11 Add the remaining fields by repeating step 9 and using one of the two methods in step 10.

12 Press F7 to exit the Mailing Address text box.

13 Choose Insert. You return to the Run Merge dialog box.

14 Choose Merge.

15 Choose File, Print/Fax; or press Shift+F7. This prints the merged form letter and an envelope for each letter.

Numbering

Numbers lines, paragraphs, pages, and chapters for you.

Line Numbering

Numbers lines in your document automatically and then updates the numbers if you move the text.

To turn line numbering on

1 Place the cursor where you want to start numbering lines in your document.

2 Choose Layout, Line; or press Shift+F8, Line. The Line Format dialog box appears.

3 Choose Line Numbering. The Line Numbering Format dialog box appears.

4 Select the Line Numbering On check box.

5 Choose the options you want used for the line numbering.

6 Choose OK and Close as necessary to return to the document.

To turn line numbering off

1 Place the cursor where you want to turn off line numbering in the document.

2 Choose Layout, Line; or press Shift+F8, Line. The Line Format dialog box appears. Choose Line Numbering. The Line Numbering Format dialog box appears. Deselect the Line Numbering On check box.

3 Choose OK and Close as necessary to return to the document.

You do not see the line numbering in the document on-screen unless you use Print Preview. The numbers appear only in the printed document.

Paragraph Numbering

Numbers paragraphs with or without outline levels.

To number paragraphs

1 Place the cursor where you want to start numbered paragraphs in the document.

2 Choose Tools, Outline, Begin New Outline; or press Ctrl+F5, Begin New Outline. The Outline Style List dialog box appears.

3 Move the highlight bar to either Paragraph (which uses level numbers) or Numbers (which provides numbers with no level style).

4 Choose Select.

5 Type the text, pressing Enter to separate paragraphs.

6 Choose Tools, Outline, End Outline; or press Ctrl+F5, End Outline to turn off outlining.

Page Numbering

Numbers pages and prints the numbers where you specify on the page.

To number pages

1 Place the cursor at the beginning of the document.

2 Choose Layout, Page; or press Shift+F8, Page. The Page Format dialog box appears.

3 Choose Page Numbering. The Page Numbering dialog box appears.

4 Choose Page Number Position. The Page Number Position dialog box appears.

5 Choose the desired page number position and choose OK.

6 Choose the options you want used for the page numbering.

7 Choose OK and Close as necessary to return to the document.

To see how page numbers will look after being printed, choose **F**ile, Print Pre**v**iew.

See also *Print Preview.*

Outline

Creates an outline structure on which you build an outline of your document. If you later move elements of the outline to another position in the document, WordPerfect renumbers these elements for you.

Outlines often are used to organize your thoughts for a document or speech and can become the basis for a book. WordPerfect 6 offers a completely new collapsible outline feature that enables you to insert body text, copy and move outline families, hide and unhide text, or outline levels.

An *outline family* is the level identifier (for example, a bullet) of the outline item where the cursor is located, the text of the outline item, and any subordinate outline items or body text beneath the outline item.

To create an outline

1 Choose **T**ools, **O**utline, **B**egin New Outline; or press Ctrl+F5, **B**egin New Outline. The Outline Style List appears, listing a variety of outline styles.

2 Highlight a style in the list, and then choose **S**elect to return to the document.

3 Begin typing the text for the first outline level.

4 Press Enter to insert another same-level number, or press Enter, Tab to insert a lower-level number, and then type the text.

5 Press Enter, Shift+Tab to insert a higher level number (for example, to go from a second level back to a
first level).

6 Press Ctrl+T to turn off outlines temporarily so that
you can insert body text. Press Ctrl+T to turn on
outlines again.

Press Ctrl+O to edit in Outline Mode. The Outline
Bar appears so that you can access commands easily by using the mouse or the keyboard.

7 Repeat steps 3 through 6 to complete the outline.

8 To turn off the outline feature, choose Tools, Outline, End Outline; or press Ctrl+F5, End Outline.

To copy, move, or delete an outline family

1 Position the cursor on the outline family to be copied, moved, or deleted.

2 Choose Tools, Outline, and then choose Move Fam-
ily, Copy Family, or Cut Family; or press Ctrl+F5,
Move/Copy and then Move Family, Copy Family, or
Cut Family.

3 If copying, place the cursor where you want to copy
the family to your document, and then press Enter.

If moving, place the cursor at the destination, and
press Enter to insert the family.

If cutting, the outline family is deleted. After deleting
an outline family by using Cut, you can retrieve the
cut outline family by following step 2 but choosing
the Paste option. (Choose Paste or Paste, as
appropriate.)

To insert body text

1 Press Ctrl+T to temporarily turn off outlines.

2 Type the body text.

3 Press Ctrl+T to turn outlines on again.

To hide or show an outline family

1 Position the cursor on the family.

2 Choose **T**ools, **O**utline, **H**ide Family; or press Ctrl+F5, **H**ide/Show, –Hide Family. The subordinate levels of the family are hidden.

3 To unhide the subordinate levels of the family, position the cursor on the hidden family. Choose **T**ools, **O**utline, **S**how Family; or press Ctrl+F5, **H**ide/Show, +Show Family. The subordinate levels of the family are displayed.

Experiment with the different outline styles and the new features in a blank document until you are comfortable using them.

See also *Styles.*

Page Breaks

Controls where one page ends and the next begins.

Page breaks show you where one page ends and another begins. After you fill up one page and are ready to start another, WordPerfect inserts a *soft page break* that appears as a single line. If you add or delete text on a page, WordPerfect recalculates the soft page break for you and moves the soft page break code to the appropriate position.

A *hard page break* is one you have forced to occur in the document. A hard page break appears as a double line in your document. This type of page break is useful if you want a new topic to begin on a new page.

To manage page breaks

1 Type Ctrl+Enter to end a page and begin a new one.

This inserts a hard page break.

2 Delete page breaks by opening Reveal Codes, placing the cursor on the [HPg] code in your document, and then pressing Del.

Other ways to control page breaks are to use the Block Protect function, Widow and Orphan protection, or the Conditional End of Page command.

Block Protect

Prevents a block of text from being split in two by a soft page break. If protected, the entire block moves to the next page, after the page break. You may use block protect on text or graphics boxes.

To protect a block of text

1 Select the block of text.

2 Choose **L**ayout, **O**ther, **B**lock Protect; or press Shift+F8, **O**ther, **B**lock Protect.

3 Choose OK and Close as needed to return to the document.

Widows and Orphans

Prevents widows and orphans by holding at least two lines of text together on a page.

A *widow* is the first line of a paragraph that begins on the last line of a page; an *orphan* is the last line of a paragraph that begins on the first line of a page. Turning on widow and orphan protection ensures that these types of breaks do not occur.

To turn on widow and orphan protection

1 Place the cursor where you want the protection to begin.

2 Choose **L**ayout, **O**ther, **W**idow/Orphan Protect; or press Shift+F8, **O**ther, **W**idow/Orphan Protect.

3 Choose OK and Close as needed to return to the document.

Reminder

To turn on Widow/Orphan protection for documents you create in the future as well as the current document, choose **L**ayout, **D**ocument, Initial Codes Setup. The Initial Codes Setup dialog box appears. Follow steps 1 through 3 above.

Conditional End of Page

Keeps a specified number of lines together on a page.

To turn on conditional end of page

1 Count the lines you want to keep together on the same page.

2 Place your cursor at the beginning of the line just before these lines.

3 Choose **L**ayout, **O**ther, **C**onditional End of Page; or press Shift+F8, **O**ther, **C**onditional End of Page. The Other Format dialog box appears, and the cursor is placed in the Number of Lines to Keep Together text box.

4 Type in the text box the number of lines you want to remain together.

5 Choose OK and Close as needed to return to the document.

Paper Size/Type

Enables you to choose different types and sizes of paper appropriate to the current project.

WordPerfect enables you to print on several different sizes and types of paper, depending on what your printer can handle. You can print memos on half-sized sheets, for example, or legal forms on legal-sized paper. The types of paper and their sizes are called *paper definitions*. After you set up these definitions, you can choose them as necessary.

To select paper definitions

1 Place the cursor where you want to change paper size or type in the document. (If Auto Codes are on, this can be anywhere in the page, and the code is moved to the beginning of the page.)

2 Choose **L**ayout, **P**age, Paper **S**ize/Type; or press Shift+F8, **P**age, Paper **S**ize/Type. The Paper Size/ Type dialog box appears.

3 Move the highlight bar through the Paper Name list to the desired paper definition. Then choose **S**elect.

4 Choose OK and Close as needed to return to the document.

If you do not see the paper definition you want, you can add it to the Paper Size/Type dialog box.

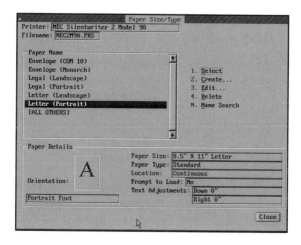

To add a paper type

1 In the Paper Size/Type dialog box, choose the [ALL OTHERS] Paper Name. The All Others dialog box appears.

2 Choose your paper type from the Paper **T**ype pop-up list.

3 Choose your paper size from the Paper **S**ize pop-up list.

4 Choose OK to enter your choices into the document. The Page Format dialog box reappears.

5 Choose OK and Close as needed to return to the document.

Password Protecting Your Documents

Keeps documents confidential by enabling you to assign a password to files.

To set or remove a password

1 Open or retrieve the file you want to password-protect.

2 Choose **File**, Save **As**; or press F10. The Save Document dialog box appears.

3 Press Password (F8) to password-protect the file. The Password dialog box appears.

4 Type your password, and choose OK. WordPerfect asks you to reenter the password.

5 Retype the password for verification, and choose OK again. The Save Document dialog box reappears.

6 Choose OK to save the document, which now is password protected. Each time you open the document, a Password dialog box appears, and you must enter the document password.

7 To remove the password, open the document. Choose **File**, Save **As**; or press F10. The Save Document dialog box appears.

8 Press Password (F8). The Password dialog box appears.

9 Press Remove (F6). The Save Document dialog box reappears.

10 Choose OK to save the document with the password removed.

Passwords aren't case-sensitive and therefore can be typed using either upper- or lowercase letters.

Use this feature with caution. If you lose or forget the password, not even WordPerfect can open the file for you again.

Print

Prints a document by using the settings you choose for your printer and fonts.

To print a document

1 Choose **File Print**/Fax; or press Shift+F7. The Print/Fax dialog box opens.

2 Change the settings as required.

3 Choose **Print** to print the document.

The following list shows choices available in the Print dialog box.

Settings	Action
Select	Takes you to the Select Printer dialog box so that you can choose another printer driver.
Full Document	Prints the entire document.
Page	Prints the page displayed on-screen where the cursor is located.
Document on Disk	Opens the Document on Disk dialog box so that you can type the file name for a document saved on disk and then prints the document without opening it.
Multiple Pages	Opens the Print Multiple Pages dialog box to enable you to specify the page numbers to print.
Blocked Text	Prints selected text and graphics in a document.

continues

Settings	Action
Control Printer	Opens the Control Printer dialog box to enable you to check the status of jobs printing or waiting to print. From this dialog box, you also can cancel and rush print jobs.
Print Preview	Shows you what the document will look like after printing, including graphics (if your monitor can display them). Footers, headers, footnotes, endnotes, page and line numbers, and justification all appear on-screen.
Initialize Printer	Opens a dialog box containing a Continue/Cancel prompt, asking if you want to proceed with this option. If you answer Continue, soft fonts (if available) are downloaded to your printer.
Fax Services	Enables you to directly fax a WordPerfect document by using a fax modem. (See also *Fax*.)
Print Job Graphically	Improves the quality of certain printing projects such as light text or images that are over a dark background.
Number of Copies	Enables you to specify the number of copies to print.

Settings	Action
Generated by	Chooses whether multiple copies are generated by WordPerfect or the printer. If your printer supports it and you choose to have multiple copies generated by the printer, WordPerfect sends a page and then a command to the printer to print the number of copies of the page you have requested. You must manually collate the pages after they have printed.
Output Options	Enables you to choose how your print job comes out of your printer and is collated. This option is only available for printers that support output bin options.
Text Quality	Offers a choice of High, Medium, Draft, or Do Not Print. Draft is faster, but High produces the best-looking printout.
Graphics Quality	Offers a choice of High, Medium, Draft, or Do Not Print. High gives the best graphics resolution, but Draft is faster.
Print Color	If you have selected a printer that can print in color, you can choose to print in color or only with black ink.

continues

Settings	Action
Print	Prints the document according to current Print dialog box settings.
Close	Closes the Print dialog box without printing the document.

Hint

Use the Print button on the Button Bar to print a document with a click of the mouse.

Print Setup

Enables you to change printer settings according to the needs of the document printed. Print settings set up in Print Setup are permanent settings that you can temporarily override for individual documents by using the Print dialog box, as discussed in the preceding section.

To set print preferences

1 Choose File, **Print**/Fax; or press Shift+F7. The Print/Fax dialog box appears.

2 Choose Setup (Shift+F1). The Print Setup dialog box appears.

3 Change options as appropriate for your documents.

4 Choose OK to accept the choices and close the box.

The following list describes some of the choices you can make in the Print Settings dialog box.

Option	Action
Number of Copies	Enables you to specify how many copies to print.
Generated By	Chooses either WordPerfect or your printer for multiple copies (if your printer supports this option).
Text Quality	Determines the resolution of printed text and whether text is to be printed.
Graphics Quality	Determines the resolution of graphics and whether they are to be printed.
Print Color	If you selected a printer that can print in color, you can choose to print in color or only with black ink.
Redline Method	Specifies appearance and placement of Redline markings.
Redline Character	Enables you to select the character to be used if you select a Redline Method that places a redline character in the left or right margins of the document.
Baseline Placement for Typesetters	Selecting this check box puts the baseline of the first line of text at the top margin rather than under the top margin.
Threshold Point Size	This setting determines when WordPerfect will send letters to the printer as a graphic instead of a text character. Printing large characters graphically sometimes results in better resolution of the character.

As WordPerfect generates the copies, it creates and then sends to the printer enough copies of the print job to meet the number you set. This method produces a print job for which all the papers are collated, but it takes longer to print. If the printer supports multiple copies, WordPerfect sends one print job to the printer and tells the printer to make a set number of copies. In this case, pages are not collated, but print time is faster.

Print Control

Enables you to track the progress of a print job after you send it to the printer. Print Control also enables you to stop a print job so that you can start a rush printing job and then reprint the interrupted job after the rush job prints.

To access the Control Printer dialog box

1 Choose File, Print/Fax; or press Shift+F7. The Print/Fax dialog box appears.

2 Choose Control Printer. The Control Printer dialog box appears.

To cancel a print job

1 Access the Control Printer dialog box as described in the preceding steps.

2 Move the highlight bar to the job you want to cancel.

3 Choose Cancel Job. A Yes/No dialog box appears. Choose Yes to cancel the job.

To stop the current print job

1 Access the Control Printer dialog box as described previously.

2 Choose Stop.

3 To restart the interrupted print job, choose Go. The job restarts from the beginning.

To rush a job in the print queue

1 Access the Control Printer dialog box as described previously.

2 Select a job in the queue, and choose **R**ush Job. A **Y**es/**N**o dialog box appears.

3 Choose **Y**es to rush the job. The selected job is moved to the top of the print queue and prints next. If you stop and restart the printer from the Control Printer dialog box, the rush job begins printing.

Print Preview

Shows you what the document will look like after printing, including graphics (if your monitor can display them). Footers, headers, footnotes, endnotes, page and line numbers, and justification all appear on-screen.

To preview your document

1 Place the cursor where you want to begin viewing the document.

2 Choose **F**ile, Print Preview; or press Shift+F7, Print Preview. The document appears on-screen as it will print.

3 Choose an option from the Button Bar, such as Zoom 100% or Full Page, to preview the document. If the option you want isn't on the Button Bar, choose the option from a menu.

4 Choose Close to return to the document.

The list that follows describes the options available on the Print Preview **V**iew menu.

Option	Function
100% View	Displays the page at actual size.
200% View	Displays the page at twice the actual size.

continues

Option	Function
Zoom In	Enlarges the displayed image for closer examination of the document.
Zoom Out	Reduces the displayed image to see more of the document. Enables you to better see how the page is formatted.
Zoom Area	Enlarges the display of a selected area up to 400%. Select the area by dragging the mouse.
Select Area	Displays a mini-representation of your document and a box representing the viewing area at the current zoom scale. Enables you to move the viewing area box to select an area in your document to view at the current zoom scale.
Reset	Resets the view and size ratios to the settings in effect when you opened the Print Preview window.
Full Page	Displays the entire current page.
Facing Pages	Displays the full-page images of two consecutive pages as they would appear in a book.
Thumbnails	Displays a miniature quick sketch of multiple pages.
Button Bar	Displays the Print Preview Button Bar (with buttons for selecting viewing options) on an edge of the Print Preview window.
Button Bar Setup	Configures a custom Button Bar for Print Preview. Works like the document editing window Button Bar options. See *Button Bars* for more details.

Before printing a document, take a look at it by using
Print Preview. Taking the time to preview documents
saves you from making mistakes and wasting printing
paper.

Printer Setup

Enables you to use the Edit Printer Setup dialog box to
change your printer settings, select cartridges and fonts,
change the initial font, specify the directory where soft
fonts are located, change the port destination, and
choose a sheet feeder and bin number if your printer is
equipped with a sheet feeder. You also can set up a
network printer port here.

To set up your printer

1 Choose File, **P**rint/Fax; or press Shift+F7. The Print/
Fax dialog box opens.

2 Choose **S**elect. The Select Printer dialog box opens.

3 Highlight the printer that you want to set up and
choose **E**dit. The Edit Printer Setup dialog box
appears.

4 Change the settings as required.

5 Choose OK and Close as needed to return to the
document.

Reminder

If you change the port destination to print
to a file on disk, make sure that you change
this setting back after printing. Otherwise,
all print jobs continue to print to this file.

See also *Fonts* and *Print Setup*.

QuickMarks

Places a QuickMark in the document to hold your place so that you can return to that location quickly.

To place a QuickMark

1 Place the cursor where you want a QuickMark.

2 Choose Edit, Bookmark; or press Shift+F12. The Bookmark dialog box appears.

3 Choose Set QuickMark; or press Ctrl+Q. The QuickMark is inserted into your document, and the dialog box closes.

To find a QuickMark

1 Choose Edit, Bookmark; or press Shift+F12. The Bookmark dialog box appears.

2 Choose Find QuickMark; or press Ctrl+F. You return to the document at the place where the QuickMark is set.

To turn off automatic QuickMarks

1 Choose Edit, Bookmark; or press Shift+F12. The Bookmark dialog box appears.

2 Deselect the Set QuickMark in Document on Save check box to turn off this option. (It is on by default.)

By default, WordPerfect puts a QuickMark at the current cursor location whenever you save a document.

See also *Bookmarks*.

Reveal Codes

Shows you what formatting codes are inserted in the document and where they are located.

For many of WordPerfect's formatting codes, if you view them with the Reveal Codes window open, the value of the code and detailed formatting information is not shown. If you move the cursor to the code, it expands and shows the detailed formatting information. For example, a [Lft Mar] code that sets the left margin to 2 inches expands and shows [Lft Mar:2"]. The default is not to display the detail of formatting codes, but you can set WordPerfect always to display the formatting detail in the Reveal Codes window.

To use Reveal Codes

1 Choose View, Reveal Codes; or press F11 or Alt+F3.

   Your screen splits in two, with some of the document displayed in the top part and the hidden codes in the same text displayed in the bottom part.

2 To close Reveal Codes, choose View, Reveal Codes; or press F11 or Alt+F3.

Reminder

You also can toggle Reveal Codes on and off by pressing Alt+F3. The fastest way to turn Reveal Codes on and off, however, is to place a Reveal Codes button on the Button Bar.

WordPerfect 6 is a WYSIWYG ("what you see is what you get") word processor, so codes are not visible on-screen as you type. If you make a mistake in typing and place the wrong code in a document—or place the right code in the wrong place—you can use Reveal Codes to see the code and delete it. Learning to use Reveal Codes saves you from trouble as you edit a document.

To use Reveal Codes to delete a formatting code

1 With the Reveal Codes window open, place the mouse pointer on the code you want to delete, and click the left mouse button. Hidden codes appear in the Reveal Codes part of the screen and are enclosed by brackets.

2 The code you selected is now highlighted. To remove the code, press Del.

To change the size of the Reveal Codes window for the current session

1 Choose View, Screen Setup; or press Ctrl+F3. The Screen dialog box appears.

2 Choose Reveal Codes, Window Percentage.

3 Type the percentage of the screen you want devoted to the Reveal Codes window.

4 Choose OK to return to the document.

To permanently change the size of the Reveal Codes window

1 Choose View, Screen Setup; or press Ctrl+F3, Shift+F1. The Screen Setup dialog box appears.

2 Choose Reveal Codes, Window Percentage.

3 Type the percentage of the screen you want devoted to the Reveal Codes window.

4 Choose OK to return to the document.

To display codes in expanded detail

1 Choose View, Screen Setup; or press Ctrl+F3, Shift+F1. The Screen Setup dialog box appears.

2 Choose Reveal Codes, Display Details. Selecting this check box causes WordPerfect to display expanded codes with detailed formatting information. Although some codes are now always expanded in the Reveal Codes window, other codes still require that the cursor be moved to them before they expand and show detailed formatting information.

3 Choose OK until you return to the document.

4 To return to nonexpanded codes, repeat these steps and deselect the Display Details check box.

Ribbon

Saves time by enabling you to change the screen display zoom ratio, apply styles, change fonts, point sizes, and justification in the document. The Ribbon also can turn on newspaper columns and enable you to choose the number of columns. You must use a mouse to use the Ribbon.

To display the Ribbon

- Choose View, **R**ibbon to display the Ribbon in the document for the current document.

- Choose View, Screen Setup, **S**creen Options, and either **R**ibbon (Graphics) or R**i**bbon (Text) to display the Ribbon in all documents as a permanent part of the window. Graphics and Text refer to the screen display mode. You can choose to always display the Ribbon in one mode and not the other.

To use the Ribbon

To use the Ribbon, choose from these options:

- Click the Zoom button to choose a new Zoom percentage from the drop-down list if you are in Graphics Mode or Page Mode.

- Click the Style button to choose and to apply a defined style to your document.

- Click the Columns button to choose and to turn on the number of columns.

- To change justification, click the Justification button.

- To change the font, click the Font Style button.

- To change the font's point size, click the Point Size button.

Changes made with the Ribbon are temporary and remain in effect until you change them or until you start a new document.

Save As

Enables you to save a document under a new name, in a new format, or in a different directory from the default document directory.

To use Save As

1 Retrieve a document or create a new one.

2 Choose **File**, Save **As**; or press F10. (You also can click the Save As button on the Button Bar.)

3 In the Save As dialog box, type the file name in the text box.

4 To save the file in a different format, choose the format you want from the pop-up list of the Format text box.

5 To save the file in another directory, type the drive and directory information before the file name in the text box.

6 Choose OK or press Enter to save the file.

Reminder

Choosing Save replaces the original copy of the file on your drive with the document on-screen if both have the same name. Choosing Save As enables you to rename the file so that you retain the original version while saving the new one.

If you Choose Close or Exit without saving a document first, WordPerfect asks if you want to save the file.

Hint

Put Save As on your Button Bar to save time.

Search and Replace

Instantly finds and replaces text and codes in a long document.

To search for text or codes

1 Place the cursor in your document where you want to begin the search.

2 Choose Edit, Search; or press F2. The Search dialog box opens. Press Shift+F2 to display the Search dialog box with the Backward Search option selected.

3 Choose search options in the dialog box, including whether to search forward or backward.

4 Type the word, phrase, or text for which you want to search.

5 Choose Codes (F5) if looking for a code, and scan the codes list. Choose the code in question, and choose Select to put the code in the Search For text box.

Many codes can be entered by simply pressing the keys or function key combination that selects the feature. For example, to search for the [Bold On] code, press F6 to quickly insert the code into the Search For text box.

Choose Specific Codes (Shift+F5) to search for codes with a specific value: for example, a code that sets the left margin to two inches. When you choose the code, a code-specific dialog box opens in which you type the value for which you want to search. Choose OK to insert the code and value into the Search For text box.

6 Press Search (F2) to begin the search.

Search stops at the first instance of the item. You can Search for other occurrences of the word or code by pressing F2, F2 to search for the next occurrence or Shift+F2, F2 to search for the previous occurrence.

To replace text or codes

1 Choose **E**dit, Rep**l**ace; or press Alt+F2. The Search and Replace dialog box appears.

2 Type the word, phrase, or text you want to replace and the text you want to use as a replacement in the respective text boxes.

To replace the Search For item with nothing, press Tab after pressing Del, which deletes all text in the Replace With text box.

3 Choose search and replace options in the dialog box, including whether to search forward or backward and whether you want to confirm each replacement.

4 Choose Replace (F2) to begin the replacement. If you have checked the Confirm Replacement check box, WordPerfect displays a Confirm Replacement dialog box in which you can choose **Y**es to replace the current item, No to bypass the current item, or **R**eplace All to replace all further occurrences of the item.

5 To replace a code, choose Codes (F5) or Specific Codes (Shift+F5). Scan the codes list, select the code you want to replace, and choose Select to put the code in the Replace text box.

If you select Specific Codes, a code-specific dialog box opens. This dialog box contains text boxes in which you enter the value of the code you want to search for and the value with which to replace the found item. Choose Search and Delete (F4) to find codes with a certain value and delete them.

Reminder

You can replace a word with nothing by typing the word to replace in the Search For text box, leaving the replacement text box blank, and then choosing Replace (F2).

Select

Selects or defines a portion of text for deletion, moving, copying, or perhaps enhancing with bold or underline. Selected text appears as highlighted text.

To select by using the mouse

1 Place the cursor at the beginning of the text you want to select.

2 Hold down the left mouse button and drag through the text until you reach the end of the text to highlight.

3 Release the mouse button. The text now is selected and marked with a highlight.

Reminder

If you change your mind, just place the cursor anywhere within the selected text and click the left mouse button once to cancel the selection. To delete the selected text, just press Del.

The following list shows some shortcut mouse tricks for selecting text.

- Double-click selects a word.

- Triple-click selects a sentence.

- Quadruple-click selects a paragraph.

- After text is selected, Shift+click extends the selection to the position of the pointer.

See also *Block*.

You also can use Select with Block Protect to keep the selected portion together on a page during editing.

The easiest method of selecting text is to drag the mouse through the text.

Drag and Drop Text

Enables you to move or copy selected text from one part of the document to another by placing the cursor on the selected text, holding down the left mouse button, and then dragging the text to the new location.

To drag and drop

1 Select text to be moved or copied.

2 Put the cursor anywhere in the selected text.

3 Click the left mouse button and hold it while moving the mouse to a new location in the document. The mouse pointer icon changes to indicate that the selected text is attached to the mouse pointer.

4 Normally, the selection is *moved* to the location of the mouse pointer when you release the mouse button. Press and hold Ctrl while releasing the mouse button to *copy* the selected text to the new location.

5 If you change your mind, move the mouse pointer back into the highlighted selection before you release the mouse button.

Block

Highlights a section of text for editing or formatting.

To block text by clicking with the mouse

1 Place the cursor at the beginning of the text to be blocked.

2 To block the word, double-click the mouse button. To block the sentence containing the word, triple-click the mouse button. To block the paragraph containing the word, quadruple-click the mouse button. WordPerfect displays the Block On message at the lower-left edge of the status line.

3 Perform the editing or formatting task on the block.

To block by dragging with the mouse

1 Move the screen pointer to the first character or formatting code you want included in the block.

2 Click and hold the mouse button while dragging the screen pointer to the last character or formatting code you want included in the block. WordPerfect displays the `Block On` message at the lower-left edge of the status line.

3 Release the mouse button.

4 Perform the editing or formatting task on the block.

To block by using the keyboard

1 Move the cursor to a location adjacent to the first character or formatting code that you want included in the block.

2 Choose **E**dit, **B**lock; or press F12 or Alt+F4. WordPerfect displays the `Block On` message at the lower-left edge of the status line.

> ### Shortcut
>
> Press Ctrl+F4 to display the Move dialog box, and choose **S**entence, Pa**r**agraph, or P**a**ge. The program automatically highlights the designated amount of text at the cursor's location.

3 Use any cursor-movement key—arrow key, PgUp, PgDn, Home+arrow key, End, + (on the number pad), – (on the number pad), Ctrl+arrow key, and so on— to move the cursor to a location adjacent to the last character or formatting code to be included in the block.

> ### Shortcut
>
> If the program displays the `Block On` message, you can expand the area highlighted in the block by using the Search (F2), Backward Search (Shift+F3), or GoTo (Ctrl+F3) features. You also can expand the highlighted area by typing a character or pressing any key combination that inserts a formatting code for a WordPerfect feature.

4 Perform the editing or formatting task on the block.

Block Protect

Keeps a highlighted text block together on one page. Use Block Protect to keep lines of text, a table, or chart from wrapping across two pages.

To protect a block of text

1 Using one of the methods described in the preceding section, block the text to be protected.

2 Choose **L**ayout; or press Shift+F8. Choose **O**ther, **B**lock Protect. The program inserts a [Block Pro On] code at the beginning of the text block and a [Block Pro Off] code at the end of the block.

3 Choose OK to close the dialog box and save the new settings. (If you accessed **L**ayout feature by using Shift+F8 in step 2, you also must choose Close. Alternatively, exit the Other Format dialog box by pressing Home, F7.)

Shell

Acts as a menu shell for launching WordPerfect and other programs. Using the Shell, you can go to DOS, save and retrieve information with the Clipboard, perform DOS commands, and send a document as a mail message. You also can switch from program to program without exiting.

To go to DOS

1 Choose **F**ile, **G**o to Shell; or press Ctrl+F1. The Shell dialog box opens.

2 Choose Go to DOS.

3 At the DOS prompt, type **exit** and press Enter to return to WordPerfect.

To use the Shell Clipboard feature

1 Choose **F**ile, **G**o to Shell; or press Ctrl+F1. The Shell dialog box opens.

2 Choose **C**lipboard Number.

3 Specify a number for the Clipboard. The Word-Perfect Shell program enables you to use up to 80 separate Clipboards numbered from 0 to 79.

4 Select the text to copy or append to the Clipboard.

5 Choose **F**ile, **G**o to Shell, or press Ctrl+F1. The Shell dialog box opens.

6 Choose **S**ave to Clipboard. The selected text is copied to the Shell Clipboard, and you return to the document.

Choose **A**ppend to append the information to the Shell Clipboard.

Choose **R**etrieve to retrieve the information saved to the Shell Clipboard to the location of the cursor in the document.

Write down the number of the Clipboard you entered in step 3 so that you can retrieve the information later.

See also *Clipboard* (*Copy*, *Paste*, and *Append*).

Sort

Sorts numbers or words in either ascending or descending order.

To sort document contents

1 If you plan to sort part of a document, first open the document you want to sort. Then select only the text you want to sort. If you want to sort an entire file saved on disk, you don't have to open the document.

2 Choose Tools, Sort; or press Ctrl+F9, Sort. The Sort (Source and Destination) dialog box appears on-screen.

3 Choose the From (Source) location of the information you want to sort, either Document on Screen or File. Then choose the To (Destination) location where you want to place the information after it has been sorted, either Document on Screen or File.

4 Choose OK. The Sort dialog box opens.

5 Choose the correct Record Type.

6 Choose Sort Keys (Sort Priority) and Add to add new keys that you want to include in the sort, Edit to edit an existing key, or Insert to insert a new sort key between existing keys. The Edit Sort Key dialog box opens.

7 Fill in the text boxes with the numbers that show WordPerfect the location of the line, field, word, or cell within the record as appropriate. Also indicate the sort Type and Order. Choose OK to return to the Sort dialog box.

8 To delete a sort key, choose Sort Keys, highlight the key to delete, and choose Delete.

9 Choose Select Records to enter criteria to use to select which records to include in the destination location. If you select this option, you also can select the Select Without Sorting check box. If you select this second option, records from the From location are not sorted but are selected and placed into the To location.

10 By default, all of the items beginning with the same letter sort together, regardless of whether that letter is uppercase or lowercase. Choose Sort Uppercase First to sort all uppercase letters before any lowercase letters.

11 Choose Perform Action to perform the sort.

This feature works with lines, paragraphs, rows in a table, or merge data file records. You can sort alphabetically or numerically, in ascending or descending order. Sort your address list, for example, alphabetically by last name, starting with the A's. For mass mailings, sort the address list by zip code to take advantage of the discount presort rate.

Reminder

You must place the cursor within a table in order to sort table contents.

Sound Clips

Enables the embedding of a sound clip in letters, memos, or spreadsheets. You also can use sound clips to create multimedia documents for presentations. You must have a sound card installed in your computer to use this feature.

To set up sound

1 Choose Tools, Sound Clip, Sound Setup; or press Ctrl+F7, 5, Shift+F1. The Sound Setup dialog box opens.

2 Choose Type. The Setup Sound Type dialog box opens. Select the sound device on your computer, and then choose Select.

3 Choose Hardware Setup. The Hardware Setup dialog box opens. If necessary, change settings to match your sound card and choose OK.

4 Choose Recording Quality Setup. The Recording Quality Setup dialog box opens. Choose options and choose OK.

5 Choose Close and OK until you return to the document.

To record dictation

1 Press Ctrl+D. The Recording Sound Clip dialog box appears.

2 Choose **O**ptions to display the Sound Clip Record Options dialog box and adjust volume and recording quality.

3 Choose **D**esc to edit the description of the sound clip.

4 Choose **R**ec to record the sound.

5 Choose **S**top to quit recording.

6 Choose **I**nsert to insert the sound clip in the document and return to the document.

To play back the voice sound clip

1 Put the cursor in front of the sound clip in the document.

2 Press Ctrl+S. The Listen and Type dialog box opens, and the sound clip begins to play.

3 Start typing text. The text appears immediately after the sound clip.

4 Choose Play/Pause, Repeat, Rwnd, Stop, or Ffwd in the Listen and Type dialog box to control the sound clip.

5 Press F7 to return to the document.

To add a sound clip to the document

1 Choose **T**ools, Sound **C**lip, **A**dd; or press Ctrl+F7, **S**ound Clip, **A**dd Clip. The Add Sound Clip to Document dialog box opens.

2 Type the file name for the sound clip in the text box.

3 Choose **D**escription, and type a description of the sound file.

4 Choose **L**ink to File on Disk to store the sound clip separately, or choose **S**tore in Document to store the sound clip as part of the document.

5 Choose OK until you return to the document.

To play a sound clip

1 Choose **T**ools, Sound **C**lip, **P**lay; or press Ctrl+F7, **S**ound Clip. The Sound Clips in Document dialog box opens.

2 Choose a sound clip in the Clip Description list.

3 Choose **P**lay.

4 Choose OK until you return to the document.

Sound clips can be either digital audio or MIDI music.

Spreadsheet Importing

Enables you to directly import and link spreadsheet files from PlanPerfect (versions 3.0 through 5.1), Lotus 1-2-3 (versions 1A through 3.1), Excel (versions 2.1 through 4.0), Quattro Pro (versions 3.0 and 4.0), Quattro Pro for Windows 1.0, and Spreadsheet DIF.

Importing a spreadsheet places a copy of the information from the spreadsheet file into your document one time only. Linking your document to a spreadsheet enables you to update the spreadsheet information in your document to keep it current as changes are made to the spreadsheet.

To import a spreadsheet file

1 Place the cursor where you want to import the spreadsheet in the document.

2 Choose **T**ools, **S**preadsheet, **I**mport; or press Alt+F7, **S**preadsheet, **I**mport. The Import Spreadsheet dialog box opens.

3 In the Filename text box, type the path and file name of the spreadsheet file to import.

4 Specify the range of cells to import, whether the spreadsheet is to be imported as a table or text, and the range name.

5 Choose Import to import the spreadsheet and return to the document.

After you import the spreadsheet as a table, don't forget to size the table to fit between the left and right margins. Choose a landscape orientation for printing if your printer supports it.

Spreadsheet Linking

Establishes a link between the spreadsheet and the document that updates the document every time you open the WordPerfect document.

To link a document to a spreadsheet

1 Place the cursor where you want to create the link in your document.

2 Choose Tools, Spreadsheet, Create Link; or press Alt+F7, Spreadsheet, Create Link. The Create Spreadsheet Link dialog box opens.

3 Type the spreadsheet file name in the text box.

4 Specify the range of cells to import, whether the spreadsheet is to be imported as a table or text, and the range name.

5 Choose Link & Import to import the selected spreadsheet information and create a link to the spreadsheet file. Or choose Link to create the link to the spreadsheet file but not import the spreadsheet information at this time. The link is created, information is copied as requested, and you return to the document.

6 The spreadsheet data is contained between a comment box showing Link and the file name and range of the link and a comment box showing Link End.

Link Editing

Edits an existing link or modifies link options.

To edit a link

1 Put the cursor between the [Link] and [Link End] codes.

2 Choose **T**ools, **S**preadsheet, **E**dit Link; or press
Alt+F7, **S**preadsheet, **E**dit Link. The Edit Spreadsheet
Link dialog box opens, displaying information about
the current link.

3 Make any required changes.

4 Choose Link & **I**mport to update the link and import
the new data or choose **L**ink to just update the link.

Updating Links

To update links, follow these steps:

1 Choose **T**ools, **S**preadsheet, **L**ink Options; or press
Alt+F7, **S**preadsheet, **L**ink Options. The Spreadsheet
Link Options dialog box appears.

2 Choose **U**pdate All Links to instruct WordPerfect to
update all links. Or, choose Update on **R**etrieve.
Links are updated whenever you open the
document.

3 Click OK as needed to return to the document.

Styles

Simplifies time-consuming formatting chores by enabling
you to create or retrieve a style to format a header or an
entire document.

Styles are special files you can write that include formatting codes and text that affect a document. Like macros,
styles perform their magic instantly. You can use styles
to format an entire document or to center a heading and
make it bold and underlined. After you create the style,
you can save it in a style library so that you can use the
same style on other documents.

Open styles remain in effect throughout the document.
You can turn on *paired styles* at a certain point in the
text and then turn them off again as you type. (Usually,
such styles as bold, underline, center, and italic are
considered paired styles.) You can even define the Enter
key to turn off the style.

After writing a document, you may decide that you want to define some styles to act on selected portions of the text. Select this part of the text by placing the cursor before the text in question, holding down the mouse button, and dragging the mouse to highlight the text. Release the mouse button and access the Ribbon Styles menu to apply the style to the highlighted text.

You edit styles by selecting the style you want to edit in the Style List dialog box and choosing Edit. The style appears in the Edit Style dialog box. Make the changes, and choose OK to close the dialog box. (Don't forget to save the edited style.)

Document styles are the styles contained and stored within a document. Choosing From Document displays in the list box of the Style List dialog box all the styles in the document.

Personal Library styles are the styles you create or edit and save to your personal library. You can copy styles from the Shared Library to the Personal Library. You also can rename and then edit styles with different codes and text. Choosing Personal Library displays in the list box the files in the Personal Library.

Shared Library styles are the styles that exist on a network shared among several users or on a single computer shared by more than one user. Choosing Shared Library displays in the list box all the styles in the Shared Library.

To retrieve styles

1 Place the cursor in your document where you want to start styles, or select the text to which you want to apply a style.

2 Choose **Layout**, **Styles**; or press Alt+F8. The Style List dialog box opens.

3 Choose the styles to be listed as From Document, Personal Library, or Shared Library. The styles appear in the list box.

If the Personal Library or Shared Library choices are grayed and not available as choices, you have not

specified the location of these files. To specify the
default location of personal and shared style libraries, choose **F**ile, Se**t**up, **L**ocation of Files. The Location of Files dialog box opens. Choose St**y**le Files
and enter the file names and paths for your style
files. Choose OK to return to the document.

4 Choose **R**etrieve. The Retrieve Styles dialog box
opens.

5 Type the file name of the style you want to retrieve
in the Filename text box.

6 Choose OK to retrieve the styles, close the Retrieve
Styles dialog box, and return to the Style List dialog
box. The list box shows the styles you retrieved.

7 Choose Close to return to the document.

To create a style

1 Choose **L**ayout, **S**tyles, or press Alt+F8. The Style
List dialog box opens.

2 To save the style in a library, choose Personal
Library or S**h**ared Library.

3 Choose **C**reate to open the Create Style dialog box.

4 Choose Style **N**ame and type the style name. Make
sure that you choose a unique file name to keep
from overwriting another style that has the same
name.

5 Choose Style **T**ype and indicate whether the style is
to be a **P**aragraph Style, which affects the paragraph
containing the cursor, a **C**haracter Style, which affects blocked text or text you are about to type, or
an **O**pen Style, which affects text from the location
of the cursor to the end of the document.

6 Selecting **C**reate From Current Paragraph enables
you to create the style from the font attributes of
the current paragraph or character.

7 Choose OK. The Edit Style dialog box opens.

8 Choose **D**escription and type a description for the
style.

9 Choose Style Contents, and then choose menu items or press keystrokes to insert formatting codes and text. Press F7 after you are done. The Edit Style dialog box reappears.

10 If you want certain formatting codes to take effect after the style ends, choose Show Styles Off Codes. WordPerfect displays a comment in the Style Contents section of the Edit Style dialog box. Choose Style Contents and enter the codes below the comment.

11 Choose Enter Key Action. The Enter Key Action dialog box opens. Define how the Enter key acts with styles. Choose OK to save changes and return to the Edit Style dialog box.

12 Choose OK. The Style List dialog box reappears and your newly created style is added and highlighted in the list box. The new style also is in the pull-down menu of Styles on the Ribbon.

13 Save the new style by choosing Save.

14 Highlight the style and then choose Select to turn the style on if you want to use the style right away. You return to the document. Choose Close to return to the document without turning the style on.

To use a style

1 Place the cursor at the start of the document to apply the style to the entire document.

To use a Paragraph Style, place the cursor in the paragraph you want to apply the style to.

To use a Character Style, place the cursor where you want the style to begin or use Block to highlight text to apply the style to.

2 Choose Layout, Styles; or press Alt+F8. The Style List dialog box opens.

3 Choose the style you want to use, and then choose Select. The style is applied to the document and you return to the document.

4 Use Reveal Codes to see the style codes.

To edit a style

1 Choose **L**ayout, **S**tyles; or press Alt+F8. The Styles dialog box opens.

2 Choose the style you want to edit.

3 Choose the Edit button to open the styles.

4 Make your changes, and then press F7 to exit.

Caution!

Make sure that Auto Code Placement is turned on if you use styles. Otherwise, style codes may not be placed correctly.

See also *Auto Code Placement.*

Subdivided Pages

Creates trifold brochures, booklets, tickets for events, programs, and so on by enabling you to create several logical pages within one physical page. WordPerfect treats each subdivided page as a separate page and numbers each page.

To set up a subdivided page

1 Make sure that Auto Code Placement is on.

2 Put the cursor anywhere on the page you want to subdivide.

3 Choose **L**ayout, **P**age and then Subdivide P**a**ge; or press Shift+F8, **P**age, Subdivide P**a**ge. The Subdivide Page dialog box appears.

4 Choose the number of columns and rows into which to subdivide the page.

5 Choose OK until you return to the document.

6 Choose **L**ayout, **P**age and then Subdivide P**a**ge; or press Shift+F8, **P**age, Subdivide P**a**ge. The Subdivide Page dialog box appears. Choose O**ff** to turn off the Subdivided Page after you finish typing the text.

To see how the text will look in the subdivided page after you print it as you compose your document, choose the Page display mode. Choose **V**iew, **P**age Mode; or press Ctrl+F3, **P**age. The physical page is shown with the subdivided pages oriented as they will print. You may need to adjust the Zoom ratio to Wide to view the page in a useful way.

See also *Zoom*.

Print as Booklet

Ensures that pages print and are numbered correctly when printing or Faxing a booklet style document.

To print as a booklet

1 Choose **F**ile, **P**rint/Fax; or press Shift+F7. The Print/Fax dialog box opens.

2 Choose **M**ultiple Pages. The Print Multiple Pages dialog box opens. Choose Print as **B**ooklet.

3 Choose OK to return to the Print/Fax dialog box.

4 Choose P**r**int. You return to the document and the document prints.

See also *Print*.

Tables

Enables you to set up tables to organize items by columns and rows without having to calculate tab settings.

Think of a *table* as a grid structure in which the text, numbers, and formulas are arranged to show their relationship to each other. A common example of this relationship is the Multiplication Table you memorized in third grade. The information is organized in *rows* (across) and *columns* (up and down). Each section of the grid is a *cell*.

WordPerfect's table feature is so powerful that you can import a spreadsheet or perform math functions in a table and let WordPerfect do the calculations. (See *Math* and *Spreadsheet Importing* for more information on these features. This section simply shows how to set up and edit a table.)

> ## Tip
>
> First decide what information you want to present in your table. The type of table you create depends on how you want to use that table. Planning ahead saves editing later.

To create a table

1 Place the cursor where you want the table to begin in your document.

2 Choose Layout, Tables, Create; or press Alt+F7, Tables, Create. The Create Table dialog box opens.

3 Type the number of columns and rows you want for the table in the appropriate text boxes.

4 Choose OK to close the dialog box. The table is created and displayed with the Table Edit menu. Choose Close to return to the document.

> ## Reminder
>
> You now can begin typing information into the table. Use Tab to move to the next cell in the row. Line wrap works within the cells so that text too long for the cell wraps to the next line of the same cell.

You can choose various table options in the Table Options dialog box.

To select table options

1 Place the cursor inside the table.

2 Choose Layout, Tables, Edit; or press Alt+F7, Tables, Edit. The Table Edit menu appears.

3 Choose Cell, Column, Row, or Table as desired, and change the settings as required.

4 Choose OK and Close to accept the new settings and return to the document.

You may want to select the percentage of gray applied to a cell if shading is chosen. Choosing 100 percent shading blacks out the cell, so be careful.

Table lines are the lines that define the rows and cells. You may edit these in the Table Lines dialog box.

To change the lines around a cell or group of cells

1 Place the cursor in the table.

2 Choose **L**ayout, **T**ables, **E**dit; or press Alt+F7, **T**ables, **E**dit. The Table Edit menu appears.

3 Choose **L**ines/Fill to open the Table Lines dialog box.

4 Choose a line type for the left, right, bottom, top, inside, or outside lines of the cells. The Line Styles dialog box opens.

5 Highlight a line style and choose **S**elect. Choose None if you want invisible lines. The Table Lines dialog box reappears.

6 Choose Close as needed to return to the document.

If you want the appearance of the table to stand out and draw attention, explore the options available in the Table Lines dialog box. You can choose a border style for the entire table, various fill percentages, and choose a color for the lines. You also can make the table cell lines invisible in this dialog box so that the data looks like parallel columns without lines.

If you have more data to include in the table, you can add more columns and rows.

To insert columns and rows in a table

1 Place the cursor where you want to add a cell in the table.

2 Choose **L**ayout, **T**ables, **E**dit; or press Alt+F7, **T**ables, **E**dit. The Table Edit menu appears.

3 Choose **I**ns. The Insert dialog box opens.

4 Choose **C**olumns or **R**ows, how many you want to insert in your table, and whether you want to insert **Be**fore Cursor Position or **A**fter Cursor Position.

5 Choose OK and Close until you return to the document.

To delete columns or rows in a table

1 Place the cursor in the row or column you want to delete.

2 Choose **L**ayout, **T**ables, **E**dit; or press Alt+F7, **T**ables, **E**dit. The Table Edit menu appears.

3 Choose **D**el. The Delete dialog box opens.

4 Choose either **C**olumns, **R**ows, or **C**ell Contents depending on what you want to delete. For columns or rows, type the desired number in the **H**ow Many? text box.

5 Choose OK and Close to make the deletion and return to the document.

You also can join two or more cells to make a bigger cell. This capability is useful for putting a title over a table.

To join cells

1 Place the cursor within the table. Choose **L**ayout, **T**ables, **E**dit; or press Alt+F7, **T**ables, **E**dit. The Table Edit menu appears.

2 Select the cells to join by dragging the mouse over the cells until they are highlighted.

3 Choose **J**oin. A **Y**es/**N**o dialog box opens. Choose **Y**es. The smaller cells now are combined into one big cell.

4 Choose OK to return to the document.

You also can divide cells to create additional cells.

To split cells

1 Place the cursor within the table. Choose **L**ayout, **T**ables, **E**dit; or press Alt+F7, **T**ables, **E**dit. The Table Edit menu appears.

2 Move the cursor to the cell you want to split. If you want to split several cells at the same time, use Block to highlight the cells.

3 Choose **S**plit. The Split Cell dialog box opens.

4 Choose either **C**olumns or **R**ows depending on what you want to split the cell into. Then, in the **H**ow Many? text box, type the desired number of columns or rows into which you want to split the cells.

5 Choose OK and Close to split the cells and return to the document.

To delete an entire table

1 From the document, use the mouse to select the entire table (including all table codes).

2 Press Delete.

To delete the table structure only

1 If it isn't already open, open the Reveal Codes window by choosing **V**iew, Reveal **C**odes; or press F11 or Alt+F3.

2 From the document, place the cursor on the [Tbl Def] code.

3 Press Delete. The table text is placed into tabular columns.

WordPerfect also offers a method of inserting and deleting rows directly from the document instead of using the Table Edit menu.

To insert a single row or column from the document

1 Place the cursor in the row where you want to add or delete rows.

2 To insert rows, choose from the following options:

Press Ctrl+Insert to insert a row above the row containing the cursor.

Press Ctrl+the keyboard plus sign to insert a row below the row containing the cursor.

3 To add a row to the end of a table, press Tab while in the last cell of the table.

4 To delete the current row, press Ctrl+Delete. A **Yes/No** dialog box opens. Choose **Yes** to delete the row.

Table of Authorities

Lists reference citations for a legal brief.

Creating a table of authorities (ToA) requires several steps:

- Decide what groupings or categories of legal citations you will have in the brief and how they should be formatted.

- Mark the first occurrence of each legal citation. Define exactly what the citation reference will say and how it will be formatted after it is printed in the ToA. This is called *marking the full form*.

- Assign a unique keyword to be associated with that particular legal reference. This is the *short form*.

- Mark all subsequent occurrences of a citation with the appropriate keyword to tie it to the full form. This is called *marking the short form*.

- Define where you want to place the ToA and what formatting options to apply.

- Have WordPerfect generate the document references (which create the ToA).

- Print the legal brief.

Marking a legal citation as a table of authorities full form

1 Select all the text for the citation that you want included in the ToA.

> **Tip**
>
> Open the Reveal Codes window to ensure that you mark exactly the text you want to include as the full form.

2 Choose Tools, Table of Authorities, Mark Full. The ToA Full Form dialog box appears.

The first time you mark a full form, the Section Name text box has the number 1. You can use numbers to identify the sections where the full forms are to be included or preferably make them more descriptive—such as State, Federal, or Other.

3 To enter the section name, choose Section Name. For a new section or if you want to for existing sections, type the name.

Alternatively, you can choose from a list of existing section names. Choose List Sections (F5). The ToA Sections dialog box appears. Move the highlight bar to the desired section name (or number) where this citation is to be included. Choose Select. You return to the ToA Full Form dialog box with your selection entered in the Section Name text box.

4 An abbreviated portion of the citation text you highlighted is displayed in the Short Form text box. If you want to use a different short form, you can edit the short form identifier. The short form name must be unique, since it is used to relate all occurrences of the same authority.

5 To view the full form, choose Edit Full Form. The ToA Full Form editing window appears. The text you have selected in your document is placed into the text editing area.

6 Edit the citation so it appears exactly as you want it to appear in the table of authorities. Then choose Exit (F7). You return to the ToA Full Form dialog box.

You can apply text enhancement codes (such as boldface, italic, or small caps) or formatting codes (such as indent) to the full form citation.

7 Choose OK. The ToA Full Form dialog box disappears, and you return to your document.

┌─ **Caution!** ─────────────────────┐

If you edit the legal citation in your brief, the text in the full form is *not* modified. You must edit the full form to change how it appears in your table of authorities.

└──────────────────────────────────┘

Marking a legal citation as a table of authorities short form

1 Move the cursor immediately prior to the citation.

2 Choose Tools, Table of Authorities, Mark Short. The Mark ToA Short Form dialog box appears. The last short form used is displayed in the text box.

3 Enter or edit the short form if necessary and choose OK.

Alternatively, to choose from a list of existing short form names, choose List Short Forms (F5). The ToA Short Forms dialog box appears. Move the highlight bar to the desired short form name. Choose Select. You return to the Mark ToA Short Form dialog box with your selection entered in the Short Form text box.

4 Repeat steps 1 through 3 until you have marked all citations.

┌─ **Reminder** ─────────────────────┐

After you have entered the ToA full form, subsequent occurrences of the citation are marked using the ToA short form name that you associated with the ToA full form.

└──────────────────────────────────┘

┌─ **Tip** ──────────────────────────┐

Because WordPerfect keeps repeating the last short form used as the default in the Mark ToA Short Form dialog box, you may want to mark all related short forms for one citation before moving to the next. You can find each occurrence of the citation quickly by using Search (F2).

└──────────────────────────────────┘

> ## Tip
>
> The short form name must be unique for each full form but also should be descriptive to help you associate the short form with the citation full form. Try to enter enough text to make sure that the short form is unique.

Before WordPerfect can generate the table of authorities, you must define where you want the table placed. You will probably want to title the page and place headings before each section.

To define and place the table of authorities at the front of the document

1 Because a table of authorities is usually placed at the end of the table of contents, move the cursor there.

2 Press Ctrl+Enter to place a hard page break at the end of the table of contents and start the table of authorities on a new page.

3 Type a heading, and then press Enter several times to insert several blank spaces between the heading and the first section.

4 Type the heading for the first section (in this example, **Cases - State**).

5 Choose **T**ools, Table of **A**uthorities, **D**efine. The Define Table of Authorities dialog box appears.

6 Choose the section name you want to place at the current location. Use the scroll bar or arrow keys to move the selection highlight bar to the desired list. If you have a very long list, you can choose **N**ame Search to quickly locate the list name.

7 Choose **S**elect. The Define Table of Authorities dialog box disappears, and you return to your document.

8 If you have more than one type of authority, repeat the steps for creating a section heading, and repeat steps 4 through 7 for defining the location of a ToA for the other sections.

9 Press Ctrl+Enter to insert a hard page break at the end of the ToA page.

10 If the next page is your document text, restart the page number at 1 to ensure that your citations are referenced to the proper page numbers.

> ### Caution!
>
> Skipping step 10 may result in inaccurate page references, because generating the table inserts new pages into the document. The new page number setting causes WordPerfect to renumber the pages correctly.

After you choose **G**enerate, WordPerfect deletes and rebuilds any previously generated table of authorities.

To use Generate to create and update the table of authorities

1 Choose **T**ools, **G**enerate; or press Alt+F5, **G**enerate. The Generate dialog box opens.

2 Choose OK. WordPerfect generates the table of authorities along with the page numbers where the legal citations can be found.

Table of Contents

Helps you create a table of contents for a document in three basic steps.

To create a table of contents

1 Mark text to include (usually, taken from headings) by first selecting the text, and then marking it.

2 Define the list as a table of contents by pressing Alt+F5, **M**ark Text.

3 Generate the table of contents by pressing Alt+F5, **G**enerate.

Marking text is the first step in creating a table of contents.

To mark text

1 Select the first item, and then choose **T**ools, Ta**b**le of Contents, **M**ark; or press Alt+F5, Table of **C**ontents. The Mark Table of Contents dialog box opens.

2 Choose the level numbers (up to 5) for the table of contents.

You may want to use chapter headings, for example, as level 1 and subheadings as level 2.

3 Continue marking items until all headings have been marked.

A table of contents usually is found at the beginning of a document.

To place the table of contents at the front of the document

1 Place the cursor at the beginning of the document.

2 Press Ctrl+Enter to generate a hard page break.

3 Move the cursor to the page above the hard page break.

4 Type a title and press Enter several times to separate the title from the list.

These steps set the location for the table at the beginning of the document.

To define the table of contents

1 Choose **T**ools, Ta**b**le of Contents, **D**efine; or press Alt+F5, **D**efine, Table of **C**ontents. The Define Table of Contents dialog box opens.

2 Choose **N**umber of Levels and enter in the text box the number of levels you want in the table of contents (up to 5).

3 Choose **L**evel and select from the 5 numbering styles (as described in the following list).

4 Choose OK to close the Define dialog box.

Numbering Style	Options Available
1. None	No page numbers.
2. # Follows Entry	Page number follows item.
3. (#) Follows Entry	Page number in ( ) follows item.
4. # Flush Right	Flush Right page numbers.
5. ...# Flush Right	Flush Right Page numbers with dot leaders.

Set a new page number for the page immediately following the table of contents.

To set a new page number

1 Place the cursor just below the hard page break.

2 Choose **L**ayout, **P**age, Page **N**umbering; or press Shift+F8, **P**age, Page **N**umbering. The Page Numbering dialog box opens.

3 Choose Page **N**umber. The Set Page Number dialog box opens.

4 Choose New **N**umber and type **1** in the text box.

5 Choose OK and Close until you return to the document.

Finally, you are ready to generate the table of contents.

To generate the table of contents

1 Choose **T**ools, **G**enerate; or press Alt+F5, **G**enerate. The Generate dialog box opens.

2 Choose OK. WordPerfect generates the table of contents along with the page numbers where the headings can be found.

If you later make changes and additions in the document, you must regenerate the table of contents to have accurate page numbers in your table of contents.

Uppercase, Lowercase, and Initial Caps

Converts characters to uppercase, lowercase, or the first letter of each word to capitals.

To convert case

1 Select the word, phrase, or passage you want to change to a different case.

2 Choose **E**dit, Convert Case; or press Shift+F3. Then choose **U**ppercase, **L**owercase, or **I**nitial Caps.

All selected text now is converted to the case you chose.

This feature is useful if you find that you forgot to turn Caps Lock on for a section that you want in all caps.

WP Characters

Provides special characters you may not find on your keyboard but can be inserted into documents.

To add WordPerfect characters to your document

1 Place the cursor where you want the special character to appear in a document.

2 Choose **F**ont, **WP** Characters; or press Ctrl+W, to open the WordPerfect Characters dialog box.

3 Choose the Set button, and then select a character set from the list. The new character set appears on-screen.

4 Choose **C**haracters and select one of the characters in the table.

5 Choose Insert to insert the character you want in your document and close the dialog box.

See your *WordPerfect Reference Manual* for a descriptive listing of these characters and symbols.

Writing Tools

Improves the quality of your finished document by enabling you to check spelling, find and repair grammar errors, and look up synonyms and antonyms in the Thesaurus.

Speller

Spell-checks the entire document, a portion of a document, or a word or checks for certain capitalization errors and occurrences of the same word twice in a row.

To use the Speller

1 Choose Tools, Writing Tools, Speller; or press Alt+F1, Speller. (You also can click the Speller button on the Button Bar.) The Speller dialog box opens.

2 Choose the option corresponding to what you want to spell check (see the following list). The Speller starts checking based on the option selected.

- Word checks the word in which the cursor is located. After looking up the word, the Speller moves the cursor to the next word.

- Page checks the current page, regardless of the location of the cursor.

- Document checks the entire document, regardless of the location of the cursor.

- From Cursor checks the document from the location of the cursor to the end of the document.

- Look Up Word enables you to type a word to spell-check.

- **E**dit Supplemental Dictionary allows you to edit the document-specific dictionary or a supplemental dictionary.

3 If a word is not found, the Word Not Found dialog box opens. In the left half of the dialog box is a list of suggested words. In the right half of the dialog box are a variety of options. Choose an option in accordance with the following information:

- If one of the suggested alternative words is the correct spelling, press the letter next to the replacement word. The new word replaces the highlighted word in the text. If the highlighted word is capitalized, WordPerfect capitalizes the replacement word.

  If you do not see the correct spelling and the scroll bar indicates more than one list of suggestions, use the scroll bar or cursor arrow keys to scroll the list and display more alternatives. If the Speller displays the message `** No Suggestions Found **`, you must manually edit the word.

- Choose Skip **O**nce, and the Speller continues past the word but flags the word again if it occurs later in the spelling check.

- Choose **S**kip in this Document, and the Speller adds the word to the document-specific dictionary and ignores the word if it occurs again later in the spelling check. If the document is saved after using the option, the Speller always ignores the word whenever it checks this document (and only this document), even during later editing sessions.

- Choose Add to Dic**t**ionary to add the word to the supplemental dictionary. The word is accepted as correct during the rest of the current spelling check and in future spelling checks of the current or other documents.

- Choose Edit **W**ord if none of the suggested alternative words is the one you need. Edit enables you to enter the correct spelling yourself.

- After you choose Edit **W**ord, the Speller dialog box appears with the prompt `Editing Misspelled Word: Press` **F7** `or` **Enter** `to exit`, and the cursor moves to the highlighted word in the text. Make the corrections to the word, and press F7 or Enter after you finish the correction. The Speller rechecks the corrected word.

- Choose **L**ookup to look up a word you may have forgotten how to spell.

- Choose Ignore **N**umbers to prevent WordPerfect from spell-checking any words containing numbers.

4 After the Speller is done, a dialog box appears with the message `Spell Check Completed`. Choose OK to close the Speller and return to your document.

5 Save your document with the spelling corrections.

If the same word appears twice in a row, the Speller displays the Duplicate Word Found dialog box. You can skip the duplicate word, delete it, edit it, or disable duplicate word checking.

If the Speller finds a word with certain kinds of irregular capitalization, the Irregular Case dialog box appears with suggested alternatives. You can skip the word, edit it, replace it, or disable case checking.

Grammatik

Checks the grammar in the document, makes suggestions, and enables you to change incorrect grammar.

To set up Grammatik preferences

1 Choose **T**ools, **W**riting Tools, **G**rammatik; or press Alt+F1, **G**rammatik. You also can click the Grammatik button on the Button Bar. Grammatik is started and the Grammatik main menu appears.

2 Press Alt+P to open the Standard Preferences menu.

3 Choose **Writing Style** to select a specific writing style on which to base WordPerfect's grammar-checking. (The default is a general writing style). The Select Writing Style dialog box opens.

4 Choose a writing style from the list.

5 Choose Change Formality Level (F3). The Select Level of Formality dialog box appears.

6 Choose a formality level. (The default is Standard.)

7 After you finish making any changes in writing style and formality level, save the customized preference file by choosing OK until you return to the Grammatik main menu.

To grammar-check a document

1 Open or create a document on-screen.

2 Choose **Tools**, **Writing Tools**, **Grammatik**; or press Alt+F1, **Grammatik**. You also can click the Grammatik button on the Button Bar. Grammatik is started and the Grammatik main menu appears.

3 Press **I** to start checking the document in Interactive Mode.

4 Make corrections by using the shortcut keys in the menu at the bottom of the screen.

5 Press **T** to look at statistics.

6 Choose Quit to quit. You return to the document.

7 Save the modified document.

To check only part of a document, select the text to check before using Grammatik.

Thesaurus

Enables you to look up synonyms and antonyms quickly without leaving the document.

A *thesaurus* is a special kind of dictionary that contains only *synonyms* (words with the same or similar meanings) and *antonyms* (words with opposite meanings). If you need a word that expresses your meaning better than one you typed, you often can find several alternatives in the thesaurus. You also can check the list of antonyms to find words with the opposite meaning.

To use the Thesaurus

1 Position the cursor within the word you want to look up.

2 Choose Tools, Writing Tools, Thesaurus; or press Alt+F1, Thesaurus. The Thesaurus dialog box appears.

3 If the word is not found, a dialog box appears with the message Word not found. If the word is found, a list of words appears.

4 Scroll up and down in the list to select the synonym that most closely expresses your meaning.

5 Choose Replace to replace the original word with the new word and return to the document.

Reminder

You can highlight any word in the list box to place it in the Word window and look it up, too. Or, you can choose Look Up to enter any word you want to look up.

Zoom

Enables you to magnify the page at different percentage levels for easier editing. You must be in Graphics Mode or Page Mode to use Zoom.

To set up Zoom preferences

1 Choose View, Screen Setup; or press Ctrl+F3, Shift+F1. The Screen Setup dialog box opens.

2 Choose Zoom.

3 Choose Percentage, and type a percentage in the text box.

If you prefer, WordPerfect will calculate the Zoom percentage according to the following options:

Zoom Option	Action
Margin Width	Displays a complete line with a minimum of white space on the sides.
Page Width	Displays the width of a page including the margin white space.
Full Page	Displays the entire page and left and right margins. If you are viewing the document in Page Mode, the top and bottom margins are also displayed.

4 Choose OK until you return to the document.

To change Zoom percentage temporarily

1 Choose View, Zoom; or press Ctrl+F3, Zoom.

2 Choose a percentage or zoom option according to the above table.

To change Zoom percentage temporarily by using the Ribbon

1 Choose View, Ribbon.

2 Click the zoom percentage box at the left end of the Ribbon.

3 Choose a setting from the pull-down menu according to the above table.

After you set Zoom preferences, the new settings remain in effect until you change them again. You can select new Zoom settings for the current document (only) from either the View menu or from the Ribbon.

See also *Ribbon*.

Index

Find It Fast with Que's Quick References!

Que's Quick References are the compact, easy-to-use guides to essential application information. Written for all users, Quick References include vital command information under easy-to-find alphabetical listings. Quick References are a must for anyone who needs command information fast!

 To Order, Call: (800) 428-5331
OR (317) 573-2500

Debra Bell
627-1929